Long Journey Home

Lucy Lipiner

Long Journey Home

A Young Girl's Memoir
of Surviving the Holocaust

USHER
PUBLISHING

New York City, New York

Long Journey Home
A Young Girl's Memoir of Surviving the Holocaust

Usher Publishing books may be ordered from your favorite bookseller.
www.usherpublishing.com

Usher Publishing
c/o CMI
13518 L. Street
Omaha, NE 68137

ISBN: 978-1-936840-70-0 (sc)
ISBN: 978-1-936840-71-7 (Mobi)
ISBN: 978-1-936840-72-4 (epub)

LCCN data on file with the publisher

Printed in the USA

Rev. date: December 2013

10 9 8 7 6 5 4 3 2

For my parents, Abraham and Roza, thank you for teaching me to embrace and celebrate life.

For Edward, my husband and my best friend. For my dear children, Rena and Steven.

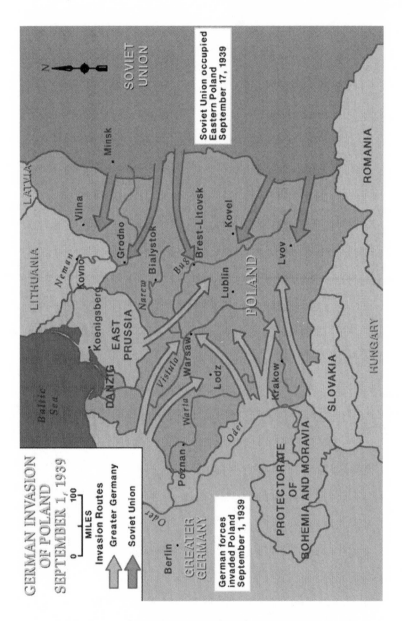

GERMAN INVASION OF POLAND SEPTEMBER 1, 1939

Courtesy of U.S. Memorial Holocaust Museum

Introduction

My old home in Sucha Beskidzka, Poland, is perhaps four thousand miles from my home in New York City. For me, it is an emotional distance that I feel apprehensive about; it is another world, another century.

My mother lost her entire family in the Holocaust. For her, it was a wound that never healed. Yet she rarely spoke of her sisters and brothers. But sometimes, I would hear her whisper, "If only I had a picture. I can't remember what they looked like."

So, in 2004, I went back to Sucha, my old home. I have no idea what I thought I'd find. The purpose of going back was not to reclaim any of her properties. As the only survivor, she was next of kin to all her siblings. No, I did not go back to make any claims on her behalf.

I went back to search for family photographs. My mother was still alive in 2004.

If I could find some family photographs, that would be better than anything, the best gift I could ever give her, I thought.

I even offered the driver a generous reward if he would also make an effort in searching for the photos. "Oh yes," he said, "I will find your pictures." Of course, he didn't.

What was I thinking? After more than sixty years, would her photos be there waiting to be claimed? I still marvel at my own thinking. Was it a little irrational, or did I experience a moment of foolish optimism?

I arrived one lovely day in the middle of summer. I lacked the courage to ring the bell. I felt uneasy, almost hoping that no one would be home. The driver came to my rescue. He rang the bell, and someone answered the door. The driver explained that someone who was born in the house wished to see it again.

The woman who opened the door was very gracious and invited me in. The old, serpentine staircase was still there. I began climbing the stairs my grandparents did so long ago, more than one hundred years. Slowly, I entered the house where I had lived the first six years of my life. The layout of the rooms was still the same. The double-paneled windows, which opened inward, were still as I remembered. Everything else was different, a little shabby and tired looking—no trace of us anywhere.

The seventy-six-year-old Maria, her arms outstretched, walked over, and we embraced. Then she just stood there looking at me. She filled in some of the missing pieces. She said she had been our neighbor before the war, and she remembered two little girls Frydzia and Lusia running around. She had been thirteen years old when World War II broke out, and she remembered that our home had been plundered almost immediately after we had left. "There was a trail of your things spilled on the sidewalks," she said.

Still looking at me, Maria said, "I have something that belongs to you." She walked over to a low cupboard and retrieved an old, yellowed envelope with my maiden name Mandelbaum written in a cursive script on top of it. Maria reached inside the envelope and withdrew an old photograph. "These are your parents. Here, it belongs to you."

I couldn't speak. I was crying. It was an old sepia photograph, dated 1927. I knew immediately it was my parents—two handsome, young people, very formal looking and wearing elegant clothes. I gathered it was my parents' engagement photograph because they were married the following year in March 1928.

Maria said she kept the photograph all these sixty-plus years because she believed someone would be coming for it someday. I was grateful to Maria for keeping the photograph. There was nothing else of ours.

Clutching the photograph, I walked over to the window. More than sixty years had melted away. For one moment, I lost all sense of time and space; there was no "now," no present time. I was a six-year-old once more. What I saw was exactly as I remembered—the market square, the rolling hills, and the beautiful Beskidy Mountains beyond. My childhood memories remained unspoiled.

I did not sense Maria's presence near me. She stood waiting for us to embrace again. I don't know what made me look for the mezuzah. Of course, it wasn't there. This time, without kissing the mezuzah, I said good-bye to my old home, knowing in my heart that I would not be coming back.

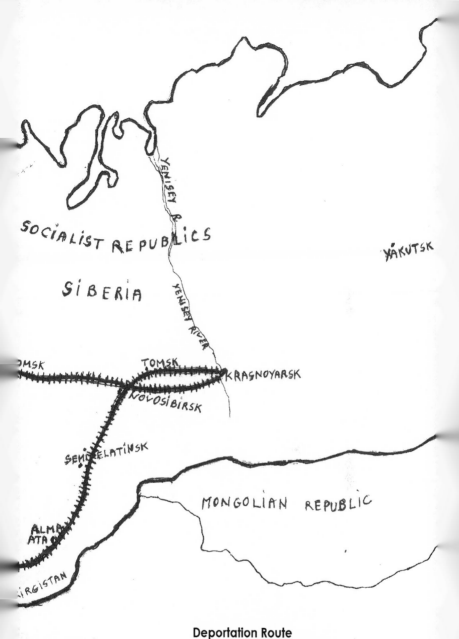

Deportation Route

Escape from the Nazis, September, 1939
Deportation to Siberia, June 1940
Resettlement in Tajiskistan, Central Asia

"He Who Saves One Life Saves the World Entire."

Talmud, Sanhedrin:37a

1
The Last Summer

The summer of 1939 turned out to be the last summer of my childhood. I had been looking forward to school. I used to look out onto the street from the wrought-iron balcony off our kitchen, my very own playground and observation post, from which I could see all kinds of activities in the streets—including the children marching off to school. I couldn't wait for school to start. On my fingers, I counted the remaining days of summer. Every day, I peeked inside my closet to touch my brand-new school uniform: navy-blue jumper with huge, white pearl buttons running down the front; white, long-sleeved shirt, starched crisp; white stockings; and blue lace-up shoes.

There was much to do that summer. My father's older sister, Tante Lotte, and her three daughters, my cousins Renee, Cecille, and Fredeke, arrived from Antwerp, Belgium. They all spoke French, Flemish, and German. We spoke Polish, Yiddish, and some German, as did everyone in Sucha. But we were able to communicate right from the start, and soon enough, our Belgian cousins had learned to speak Polish.

They brought many presents, but best of all was a pair of roller skates. Neither Frydzia nor I had ever owned a pair of roller skates; in fact, I don't think I had ever seen such skates before. Frydzia insisted that, as the oldest, she should take charge of the skates. I was devastated and wept inconsolably. So my parents came up with a fair decision: they divided the pair of skates between us. Frydzia was not happy, but I was delighted. Riding around town on one skate was pure joy. There were no automobiles in Sucha, so there was no danger of accidents.

I remember that summer of 1939 as always sunny and warm. It never rained. There was never a cloud in the sky. Was it really so? Maybe it only seems that way to me now—the bright summer days before the storm that would upend all our lives.

I remember many cousins between the ages of four and fourteen. The older ones felt much too adult to participate in our games, but it seemed we younger kids spent every minute playing. The entire town belonged to us; we could play anywhere and everywhere. We hiked. We jumped rope in the streets; the winner was the one who could keep it up the longest. We picked flowers that grew in the fields of grain on the outskirts of town. We were so busy playing that we often forgot lunch till the housekeeper came looking for us with a picnic basket.

One time, I recall running home with a handful of cornflowers. I ran straight to my father's store and into his arms.

I screamed with joy, "Look, Papa, look!"

With a big smile on his face, he picked me up, held me in his arms, and said, "Yes, yes, these flowers are beautiful like you and blue like your eyes."

As summer came to an end, Tante Lotte and our cousins prepared to return to Belgium. They left Poland on August 30, 1939, two days before the war started.

Tante Lotte; my cousins Renee, Cecille, and Fredeke; their father (my aunt's husband, Meyer); and the rest of the Jewish population of Antwerp suffered the most grievous persecution from the moment Hitler's troops entered their city in May 1940.

My aunt and my cousins would survive the war, making their way to Switzerland and safety—but not Uncle Meyer. He stayed behind in Belgium with his own father, a deeply religious man who refused to shave his beard. With the long beard, he was too obviously Jewish to be smuggled out of Belgium.

Soon enough, Meyer and his father were picked up by the Gestapo on the streets of Antwerp. They were deported east to Poland, along with thousands of other Jewish people. Uncle Meyer and his old father were killed in Auschwitz, one of the most infamous extermination camps.

2
Market Square

My hometown of Sucha (presently Sucha Beskidzka) sits in a picturesque valley of the Tatra Mountains, the highest range of the Carpathian Mountains at the junction of two rivers, Skawa and Stryszawka, Skawa being the longer of the two. In my parents' generation, Sucha was part of the Austro-Hungarian Empire; it belonged to an independent Poland when I was born. And on September 3, 1939, it became part of the German Third Reich. Before that time, however, it was home to a community of some 780 Jews—150 families, including mine.

I can still picture the old house as it stood at the edge of the market square. From the windows two flights above—for there was nothing taller than that in my town—the landscape was pleasing.

In winter, when heavy snow covered everything, you could look out on serene white streets, white rooftops, and white mountain peaks that remained undisturbed and beautiful all winter long.

Gone was the harsh sound of wheels against the cobblestones. Instead, the bells on the horse-drawn sleighs made a rhythmic ringing sound, and riding in one of those sleighs, covered snugly in heavy blankets, was pure delight. Most of all, I remember sleighing down gentle hills in the evenings under the bright light of the moon and stars with Mama and Papa, Frydzia and me between them. That was probably the best of all winter experiences.

Once the snow melted, the meadows were brilliant with flowers, and the foothills of the Tatra Mountains could be seen clearly in the distance. But sometimes, in the hazy morning light, the meadowlands and the gentle hills beyond seemed surreal in the misty setting.

On the opposite side of town, the river flowed gently, but in some places farther downstream, the rushing waters washed over small rocks and boulders and then swiftly merged with deeper water.

During warm summer days, the acacia trees provided welcome shade and serene beauty to the sunny side of our house. But most beautiful of all were the majestic chestnut trees with blossoms shaped like grapes and large, deep green leaves spread out flat, glistening in the bright sunlight.

At the edge of our town was a historical landmark—Maly Wawel, a beautiful castle that dated back to the 1500s. It had been built by an Italian goldsmith named Gaspare Castiglione for his beautiful Polish bride, Jadwiga. When I was little, the castle belonged to Count Tarnowski, a Polish nobleman.

The Tarnowski children were about my age, and I was so envious when they rode into town in a small buggy pulled by two ponies. Just as they looked for excitement in town, we looked for excitement around their castle, but we were never permitted to enter the grounds. On our hikes, all we could do was look through the elaborate wrought-iron fences to the vast lands beyond the castle—beautiful flower gardens, fruit orchards, and workers tending the fields of grain.

I remember well the house where I was born, and I remember many things that made me happy as a young child before the war. Our house of solid brick and stucco was built to last. Even as a child, I knew that the house was very old, more than one hundred years old.

Our ancestral home, center, overlooking the market square, Sucha, Poland, 1910

Our home, Sucha, 2004

It had not changed much since those days, although the acacia trees are gone, replaced by a kiosk selling newspapers, cold drinks, and picture postcards of the town. Some of the cobblestone streets had been replaced as well, paved over for the automobiles that have replaced the horse-drawn carriages and sleighs of my childhood.

I loved the house where I was born. I even loved the old, serpentine wooden stairs, worn from advanced age and hollowed out in the middle of each step by people in my family who climbed and descended those stairs long before I was born.

～～

I heard many interesting stories about my ancestors, who were born and died in the house of my childhood. They left an imprint on our lives. Sometimes, I was allowed to handle family heirlooms but only if I promised to be very careful: little silver spoons, old glass or porcelain dishes, tiny Passover wine glasses with edges decorated in gold—all handed down from my grandparents and my great-grandparents. I never knew most of my grandparents or great-grandparents; they died before I was born.

I did know my maternal grandfather, Anshel-Usher Urbach. I remember a big, beautiful house that belonged to him and his wife, my maternal grandmother, Sara Ribner Urbach.

The house was modern, with indoor plumbing—unusual in the days before the war. It stood in Kazimierz, the Jewish quarter in the old part of Krakow. Sucha, my town, was only fifty miles south of Krakow. My grandmother Sara died before I was born. Anshel-Usher was my only remaining grandparent when I was a young child. I might have seen him no more than twice in my entire childhood. But I do remember him holding me in his arms, tickling my face with his long white beard, and my arms tightly wrapped around his neck.

I remember very clearly the day my grandfather died. It was a beautiful summer day. I was five years old. I had spent the afternoon with my big sister and several friends, wading in the shallow waters of the Skawa River in our town. I remember eating blueberries and sweet cream that Frydzia and I brought from home in a large, tightly closed thermos. And I remember all of us playing a game of tossing flat little stones into the river, when our housekeeper came running.

"Come quickly," she said to Frydzia and me. "Your grandfather died, and your parents are getting ready to go to Krakow for the funeral."

I was so young and didn't understand the finality of death. Going to a big city, to a funeral, it all seemed so exciting. I wanted to go. Of course, Frydzia and I had stayed home. Funerals were not meant for young children—not in my family.

When I was a young child, I knew very little about my grandfather Anshel-Usher. Later, I learned that he was a very unusual man; he was a self-made man. People in my family loved to brag about, even to exaggerate, his great wealth. I also heard some sad stories told about my grandfather. Apparently, his widowed mother, my great-grandmother Miriam Urbach, had remarried. She had many children from her previous marriage, my grandfather Anshel-Usher being the oldest. But her new husband was unwilling to keep my grandfather under his roof, and at the age of ten, he was cast out of their home.

Anshel-Usher was apprenticed to a cobbler in exchange for food and lodging. He worked long hours, his only schooling being the cheder, the Jewish school for boys. He grew up very quickly and, early in his youth, became an entrepreneur doing a variety of jobs. He carried buckets of water from the well in the center of town to the wealthier residents. He shoveled coal into people's cellars and stoves. Life was hard for my grandfather as a young boy. But the hardships that many children endured were not unusual back in 1880, when Dickensian tales were real-life stories in many parts of Europe. In spite of—or perhaps because of—the hardships Anshel-Usher endured, he grew up to become a strong individual.

He built a large and successful business importing liquors from many parts of Europe. He built his beautiful house in Krakow. He gave much to charities, as prescribed by Jewish law. He gave to his family. They didn't lack for anything except, as my mother remembered, the one thing everyone in the family wanted most—a little love and some attention that Anshel-Usher was unable to give. Those emotions were foreign to him. He was a distant man, well spoken yet of very few words. He was always cautious—I suspect because of his very unhappy childhood.

At the beginning of World War I, he moved his entire family—my grandmother Sara, my mother, and her four siblings—to Budapest, which was then part of the Austro-Hungarian Empire. Anshel-Usher believed the family would be safer there, and he was right; the Polish people suffered grievously during the war, deprived of the most basic requirements for living, while my grandparents survived that war in relative security.

When Anshel-Usher and the family returned to the newly independent nation of Poland in 1918—when the fighting was over—they and other Jewish families of Jaworzno were greeted by a people seething with resentment over what they had suffered and ready to take out their anger on the Jews.

My mother's entire family was, at one point, almost slaughtered in a pogrom. My mother, Roza, the second youngest, was fourteen at the time. She remembered that the murderous mob ran amok, killing Jewish people and destroying property while the authorities turned a blind eye to what was happening. My mother's family, accompanied by a huge dog and a shotgun, barricaded themselves in a barn behind massive doors. Uncle Isaac, eighteen years old, was in charge of the shotgun.

As the mob was in the process of breaking down the doors, Uncle Isaac began shooting into the air, thereby upsetting the dog. The dog, crazed and barking, bit Tante Hava's leg. She was the youngest child, about twelve years old. The shooting, the barking, and the child's crying continued. Fortunately, the violent mob began to retreat, but not without consequences.

Soon, the family discovered that their home and the rest of the property were plundered and demolished. Overturned barrels of beer and many broken bottles of wine flooded the entire basement and the bar area at the street level. Huge piles of glass littered the property. Hava's leg never healed properly; it was scarred for life. But the family survived.

Anshel-Usher died in 1938, at the age of sixty-eight, one year before World War II broke out. He was spared the Holocaust and witnessing the tragic murder of four of his adult children—Hanah, Hava, Isaac, and David—and seven of his grandchildren.

The family members on my father's side lived in the house on the square for a great many years. My great-grandparents Cyla and Isaak Landerer, accompanied by a flock of youngsters— my paternal grandmother Fanny (Frymet in Yiddish) among them—came to live in the house on the square in the second part of the 1800s.

My grandfather Solomon came to live in our old house right after he and Fanny were married, when she was only sixteen years old. They had seven children. My father, the second-youngest child, was born in the house on the square in 1901, when the town was Austrian. My sister, Frydzia, and I were also born in the house on the square, but my town was no longer Austrian. Sucha became part of the newly independent and free Poland.

My father had a happy childhood. He was pampered and spoiled by his older siblings. Often, he escaped corporal punishment for misbehaving when the siblings simply created a physical barrier with their presence, thereby protecting him from his mother's anger.

My town and its tiny Jewish community had the distinction of having produced a famous person. Billy Wilder, the screenwriter and director of such films as *Sunset Boulevard* and *Some Like It Hot,* was born in Sucha in 1906. He was my father's contemporary. I heard interesting stories about the Wilder family. Billy's parents ran a restaurant in Sucha's railroad station. Billy's mother read a great deal about America; she was especially interested in the Wild West. She named her son Billy after Billy the Kid, although his real name was Samuel. The Wilder family moved to Vienna when Sucha was still Austrian.

My grandfather Solomon died of pneumonia at the age of thirty-nine. Grandmother Fanny was a young widow with the responsibility of providing for seven children. She also became a guardian of her orphaned niece Cyla and her nephew Benjamin. My father was only five years old when his father died, and being one of the youngest, he was doted upon, especially by his oldest siblings, my uncle Mehul and Tante Esther; they were like parents to him.

Life was hard for the family. It was a constant struggle for my grandmother Fanny to feed her large family. Mondays through Thursdays (Fridays she prepared for the Sabbath), Fanny got up before dawn, in all kinds of weather, and traveled by horse and buggy to many marketplaces in the surrounding countryside. She sold dress fabric, buttons, thread, and needles to farmers who came to market.

Sometimes, she bartered her goods for food that the farmers brought to market. She was able to provide only the most meager essentials, but it wasn't enough. Still, my grandmother, my aunts, my uncles, and my father never felt alone. Help was always there from family and townspeople.

I heard many interesting stories about how, on a Sabbath, the family never went without a decent meal, sometimes left anonymously at the doorstep. Looking after widows and young, orphaned children was always considered a great mitzvah, a good deed, and anonymous charity was considered the noblest form of giving.

When my father turned twenty-seven, the family found a bride for him. Although poor, he was extremely handsome. My mother—called Raisil in Yiddish—came from a wealthy family, and while she was also good looking, she was admittedly not as handsome as my father. They were married in 1928, and Mama came to live in the house on the square, which by that time had been enlarged to accommodate a large family. My mother brought furniture from Vienna, Persian rugs, hand-embroidered linens, lovely, hand-tailored clothing, and a Persian fur coat— her dowry, an important custom in that community.

Mama and Papa's engagement photograph

My parents were devoted to one another from the start, in that house on the square. Our life was totally normal—at least, that is how I remember it —until the war.

Grandmother Fanny lived with my newly married parents only one year. She died of complications from diabetes in 1929.

I never knew my grandmother Fanny. Her photograph hangs on a wall in my home and has always roused my curiosity. In the photo, she stands against a wooden fence, serene, in a dignified pose. She wears a very unremarkable woolen coat over a long, heavy cloth dress. What always appeared remarkable to me is that she is wearing a *sheitel,* a wig worn by Jewish Orthodox women, yet her facial features seem distinctly Asian. The combination of the sheitel and the Asian features is more than striking. How strange she looks—a round face, broad nose, high cheekbones, sensitivity, and quiet intelligence peeking out from the narrow, slanted eyes.

How did my Jewish grandmother, who had lived a very Jewish and sheltered life in a ghetto-like environment, inherit such un-Jewish facial characteristics? I can only speculate where our genes come from. No doubt we represent a mixture of races. Perhaps invading Mongol or Tartar warriors on horseback, pounding the earth on their way to conquer Eastern European lands, are my distant ancestors as well.

Grandmother Fanny

Purim Costume Party. Sucha, March, 1939. Lusia (front row, first on the right). Frydzia (on the right of the teacher). Syma (front row, third on the left), the only survivors. The other children and the teacher perished in the Holocaust.

3
My Town

I recall a water well in the center of town when I was a young child. Our town had no running water. From my window, I watched people pumping the water at the well, lifting and then pressing down the wooden handle several times until the water came rushing down the spigot into the old, moisture-stained, wooden pails. Sometimes, people carried modern pails of galvanized metal. My town had professional water carriers as well. Often, they carried two pails suspended from a long, wooden bar. It was hard labor; for a pittance, they delivered the water to the more prosperous residents.

When I was little, I had the natural curiosity that most children possess. I was intrigued by activities that adults were engaged in. Even simple wood chopping or splitting logs into long, flat boards fascinated me tremendously. Often, I made a nuisance of myself, asking questions, always wanting to know what came next and how things were done. Eventually I was told to go home or to "go play with your friends."

My town was a fascinating place for a young child. I loved the sights and sounds of my town that seemed almost to transport me out of the house and into the street. I loved marching and singing to lively music and bands playing old, familiar tunes. Sometimes, I'd sneak in and march and sing alongside the band players.

The most-anticipated event of all was the carousel that arrived in town every summer. What great fun my sister, Frydzia, and I had galloping round and round on top of the old, brightly painted, wooden horses.

I didn't much care for the funeral processions; a Roman Catholic horse-drawn hearse was so different from the horse-drawn wagon transporting a Jewish person in a simple, pine casket to the burial grounds. As young as I was, I recognized the differences in Jewish and non-Jewish funerals. Yet relatives, no matter their faith, mourned the departed with much the same crying, something that was very disturbing to me and always made me run home looking for Mama or Papa.

Best of all, I liked the market days, usually Tuesdays. On those days, I was out of bed with the first light in the sky. I could not sleep for fear of missing out on the most exciting adventure of all. Five groschen, my allowance, placed on my nightstand by Mama the night before, was ready and waiting to be spent at the market. I could not wait even a moment for someone in my family to help me dress. Getting dressed in the summer was easy—a dress and underwear, a pair of slipper shoes or sandals. In the winter, it was more difficult. In addition to coats, sweaters, hats, and scarves, we wore woolen stockings that were fastened to garter belts. I could not handle a garter belt.

My room had a window with a view. Early on market days, I was able to observe the first staging of the market—it was like a moving theater. From my window, I could see horse-drawn wagons full of goods and people pulling up into the square. Some vendors set up their goods on wooden stalls. Some fed their horses. It was fun to watch the horses eating their breakfast, their heads deep inside cloth bags hanging from their necks, sometimes lifting their heads and showing off mouths full of hay.

Some vendors brought dairy products to the market. The milk was not refrigerated, not pasteurized, and was often still warm. I loved the taste of that milk, and I never once got sick. The milk and kefir, the fermented milk people love in that part of the world, were ladled out into containers people brought from home.

Vendors sold household goods—white enamel cookware, inexpensive silverware, and best of all, miniature, glazed-ceramic cups and saucers. Those were my favorite and very rare purchases at the market. For the ceramic dishes, I needed to save my allowance. Mostly, I spent my allowance almost immediately; the temptation to sample candies, soda pop, and ice cream was too great.

My favorite market days were in the summer. In addition to vegetables, wild mushrooms, and wild berries, the farmers brought to town bright red and yellow cherries. But these were no ordinary cherries. These cherries were woven into circular wreaths. We called them cherry crowns. We ran around town with cherry crowns on our heads. Sometimes we played a game called cherry queen. The person who resisted eating the cherries the longest won the game. Frydzia made a practice of tempting me into eating my cherries, which was not hard at all, and seeing my crown of cherries half-eaten and hers still perched securely on her head, she delighted in teasing me. I'm the cherry queen! I'm the cherry queen!"

4
Sabbath Candles

The war came on a Friday. I know because I remember my mother setting the table with Sabbath candles. Usually, Fridays were festive and busy, with Mama and our housekeeper cooking and baking, filling the house with the most wonderful aromas—aromas that defined the Sabbath. But that Friday, Mama told the housekeeper to go back home to her village and her own family.

As the sun set, my mother lit the candles. Our home seemed strangely quiet. In the hope of preventing bombing, Sucha's residents had been ordered to avoid the use of electric lights and to paste blackout paper over the windows. The darkness felt confining. We ate our simple dinner in the dim light of the candles.

Frydzia and I were sent off to bed early. We were awakened in the middle of the night. Our clothes were neatly laid out for us. My parents said we were going away on a little vacation for a few days, a week or two at most. They had already packed our things, but they instructed us to wear layers of clothes, even though it was still summer. Frydzia and I each wore two dresses, a pair of slacks, a sweater, and a coat. I never did get to wear my school uniform. I left it hanging in the closet.

When we were ready to leave, I saw Mama looking around the house. Her gaze was drawn to the silver candelabra. She stared at it fixedly, as if she were reluctant to leave it on the cloth-covered table, as if she might be abandoning something dear to her heart.

Papa locked up the store and warehouse next door. He put on his coat and hat. Mama too wore a coat and a very elegant hat. We took turns kissing the mezuzah on the doorpost of the house. Then Papa took my hand, and Mama walked with Frydzia as we descended the serpentine stairs, not knowing it was for the last time.

5
A Day in September

Mama, Frydzia, and I stepped outside as Papa was locking up the front door of our house. To my amazement, and in spite of the darkness in the street, I could discern at least a dozen of Papa's closest relatives quietly loading their belongings into a horse-drawn wagon. I didn't understand what all these aunts and uncles and cousins were doing in front of our house.

Then I understood! This was not meant to be a vacation. In the darkness of the night, all of us were departing from our homes, in great haste and taking great care not to draw attention to our escape.

Thus began our flight eastward to what we hoped was safety. I was frightened most of the time and cried a lot. More than anything, I wanted to go back home. I didn't understand and didn't care to know what the other members of our group felt.

My father's knowledge of Nazi Germany—and, in particular, of the Nazis' hatred of the Jews—is what ultimately saved our lives. Because he had sensed that the war was imminent, he had been planning our escape even before the war started.

He persuaded his two sisters and their entire families—three generations in all—to leave their homes and businesses and join us on the difficult and at times dangerous escape. There were fourteen of us—aunts and uncles; cousins; my parents, Abraham and Roza; my big sister, Frydzia; and me.

Yet there might have been more. On the first day of our journey, Saturday, September 2, we made a stop in Bochnia, a city on the main road east, where my oldest uncle, my father's brother Mehul, and his entire family lived. My father spent half a day begging them to depart with us. But my uncle and aunt could not see it. "We have children and grandchildren," they said. "We cannot leave."

We left Bochnia and continued our eastward flight.

We were hoping to reach Soviet-occupied eastern Poland, desperately trying to outrun the German Army advancing from the west. We were traveling eastward, confining ourselves to narrow, out-of-the-way dirt roads, while the Germans with their war arsenal were everywhere, especially on paved roads.

There was not enough space in the open, horse-drawn wagon for all fourteen of us. So, early in our journey, it was decided that only the children and Cousin Bella, who was pregnant, would ride in the wagon on top of our meager belongings bundled up in sheets and blankets. My parents and the rest of the family had decided to leave the suitcases at home. They felt that bulky suitcases would be impractical in time of war. My parents, who were still in their thirties, and aunts and uncles—already in their forties—all walked beside the wagon. Sometimes, they took turns resting in a seat next to the coachman.

By the third week of our journey, everyone in the family had grown unusually quiet. Still, I was too young to know what was in their hearts and minds. I do remember sadness and tears—probably from aching bodies and the exhaustion from weeks of marching next to the wagon. I also remember sleepless nights, lack of food, poor hygiene, and the women in my family arguing over a dishpan we used to wash ourselves and our clothes at a riverbank or a stream. "Today, it's my turn." "No, it's my turn." But worst of all was the fear of getting caught by the advancing Germans. We were quite certain it would happen—that it was just a matter of time.

I remember vividly one day that September. How do you forget a feeling of being paralyzed with fear, unable to make a sound?

It was a warm day. We were caught up in a long, congested column of refugees, all fleeing eastward. The narrow dirt road was packed with horse-drawn buggies and wagons like ours. Some motor vehicles were carrying defeated Polish troops who were probably trying to get back to their families.

That day, I saw many people traveling on foot with bundles on their backs, sometimes tied to their waists or shoulders. I saw people dragging their tired children and women cradling babies in their arms, while older children clung to the edges of their mothers' dresses.

Suddenly, out of nowhere came a loud buzzing sound. Big, black, angry birds appeared on the horizon. Within moments, the black birds became a uniform squadron of flying machines high above our heads.

Pandemonium erupted around us. "German planes! German planes!" people shouted. Some began running, pushing, elbowing their way out of the crowds. Some were trampled on the ground. Some just stood and stared into the sky. In the midst of the turmoil, the sound of children sobbing was heard everywhere.

In spite of the noise around me, I heard Papa calling, "Raisil! Raisil! Run! Get away from the road! Run quick!" Mama stood a distance away. She just stood there. I'm not sure she heard him. Suddenly, I felt my hand being pulled. Papa was pushing against the crowds, dragging Frydzia and me away from the road into an open field.

Frydzia began to cry so hard that she was almost hysterical. She was crying as loud as she could. I have never heard anyone sound so desperate—"*Mamusia, mamusia!*" ("Mommy, Mommy, please come, come, please!") she screamed as she struggled with Papa, all the time trying to disengage her wrist from Papa's grip, determined to reach the place where Mama stood. But Papa persevered. We ran, and in an instant, we reached a tree thick with foliage.

Papa threw us to the ground and threw himself on top of us. It felt like a ton of bricks had fallen on top of me. I felt a choking sensation in my throat. But very soon, Papa's strong arms gave me a sense of being in a safe haven.

We remained in a tight embrace, not moving, listening to the hissing sounds of falling bombs, and the ear-splitting sounds of bombs hitting the ground, followed by an inferno of blazing explosions.

The planes disappeared from the sky. They left behind the most terrible destruction.

"We have to go back to the road and find Mama," I heard Papa yelling, trying hard to be heard above the din of explosions. But I didn't want to leave the security of our tree.

"Papa, please—I don't want to go! Please, I need to stay here," I pleaded. But he was determined to find Mama. Again he dragged us by the hand, this time back to the road. And Frydzia never stopped sobbing. "*Mamusia, mamusia,*" she kept saying over and over.

As we got closer, the scene became more unreal. People on the ground were covered in dirt and blood, their clothes torn, moaning, calling out names. Nearby was a huge crater where a bomb had exploded, dust rising high, smoke and fire everywhere. I saw a horse stretched out on the ground near an overturned carriage. An old woman, with a scarf still neatly tied around her head, seemed asleep. Yet I knew that sleep was different from any I had ever seen before. I knew the old woman was dead.

There was no sign of Mama anywhere. I had a sinking feeling in my stomach and began sobbing. Holding my father's hand, I shut my eyes for a moment. I refused to look at the injured and dead people for fear of seeing my mother among them. Papa kept calling, shouting her name over and over again.

Mama was missing, and all around us, the fires kept burning. This had to be our darkest moment of all.

It seemed like hours but was probably only minutes later that we heard Mama's voice, so faint that I could not make it out, calling to us from somewhere distant. Still holding our hands, Papa again pushed against the crowds, inching his way toward the sound of her voice, all the time calling to her, "Raisil, Raisil, we are here. Just stay where you are. Don't go away."

Surrounded by a multitude of people, there she stood like a statue. She looked strange—a ghost. Everything about her was gray. Her face was gray, her disheveled hair was gray, and her dress was covered in gray dust. She didn't speak; none of us did. We stared at her, and she stared back at us. Papa wiped his eyes with the back of his hand.

For the first time in my life, I saw my father cry. He reached out to her and quietly folded his arms around her. She barely responded. Her arms just hung there as if she could not even lift a finger to touch him. She didn't seem like my mother—she was so quiet, so indifferent. I resisted touching her; I hated to touch the dust. But Frydzia grabbed Mama's hand, holding it with one hand as she wiped away her tears with the other hand. I just stood there bewildered.

Then Papa gently drew Mama down to the ground. She began to cry. That's how I knew Mama was back.

I don't recall how the other members of our family survived the bombing. They probably ran away from the road as well. We were fortunate; we all survived another day.

6
Strange Encounter

After the terrible day of bombing, I was no longer the six-year-old I had been before—no longer a child who could believe that prayers had the power to make everything better. I understood that the people on the ground in heaps of destruction would not get up again and walk away. I understood that death was the last act of life. I became more fearful of losing my family. From that day on, I began looking over my shoulder to see if Mama, Papa, and Frydzia were still there. Sometimes, I reached out of the wagon just to hold their hands. On one occasion, I demanded to hold Papa's hat. I believed that if I held his hat, he would not ever go away and that he would be with us always.

Papa's fedora hat was my security blanket. It had always been part of him. Before the war, my father had always dressed in the most stylish and elegant clothes, completing his ensemble with a pocket watch and a chain attached to the vest of his suit and a silver-handled cane that gave a final, debonair flourish to his handsome appearance. But he always wore a hat as observant Jewish men were required to do. When I was little, he let me hold his hat, even wear it sometimes, as long as I promised to be careful. If the hat was there, it meant Papa was there. In the state of anxiety that afflicted me after the bombing, it became all-important to me.

～

Days passed. The weather was changing; it was getting colder, and it rained often. Everything was wet. This was a penetrating wetness glistening on trees and leaves, a wetness that never seemed to dry. Everyone was complaining, especially Cousin Bella. Everyone hoped she would not give birth on the road. If she did, all our efforts to escape the Nazis would have been in vain.

Polish troops were disorganized, moving in all directions. We were often stopped by Polish soldiers threatening to requisition our horse and wagon—even our coachman. Except for authorized vehicles, most cars were abandoned for lack of gasoline, so a horse and wagon seemed a useful means of transportation.

The soldiers could be menacing too. Sometimes we were ordered to show our identification papers. "Jews," they asked, "why don't you fight the Germans?" I was terrified that my father would be taken away from us. That was why I held his hat so tightly against my chest. But the fighting was over, and most people were running away. Still, these anti-Semitic sentiments openly expressed by the Polish troops intensified the uncertainty and anxiety in our lives and made my mother cry. I hated to see her cry. She did not complain much. Instead, she seemed even more vulnerable, the sadness in her eyes betraying her unhappiness. At times like that, I preferred to stay close to her. Given permission to step out of the wagon, I walked quietly by her side. I think that made us both feel better.

My father understood better than anyone the virulence of anti-Semitism. He understood that it could be deadly. He had experienced it firsthand as a young man; in fact, he had barely been a teenager. It happened one pleasant summer afternoon, on a lonely country road, when he was returning home from a nearby village. He was confronted by three young Polish men who appeared out of nowhere yelling, "Kill the Zhid, kill the Zhid!" With their fists, they beat him mercilessly. A set of large keys suspended from an enormous iron ring saved his life. Without anyone noticing anything, he reached into his pocket, withdrew the key ring, and hit one of the attackers over the head. The man screamed with pain and fell to the ground. In the brief moment that the other assailants stood bewildered and appeared disoriented, my father seized an opportunity to flee from the attackers.

Papa was the person who gave me a sense of security, if such a thing was possible under those most difficult conditions. He was sympathetic to Mama's unhappiness, but he was more interested in our physical survival than in our emotional health. My father inspired trust from the very beginning. He was the one who convinced three generations of his family to leave behind their homes and businesses to save themselves from the Nazis. Of course, he was right. His foresight saved all our lives.

My father had a wonderful sense of humor and was capable of a hearty laugh when things were funny. And despite the fragility of our existence, there were sometimes funny situations. I recall the time a decision had been made for a "bathroom" stop. While all of us little children relieved ourselves under the wagon, the adult men at once began running into the bushes, unbuckling their belts and trousers. The sight of the men running off that way struck my father as funny, and he just stood there laughing. He could see humor in the most unlikely places and situations. It was, I think, his best trait—the source of the optimism that kept him going and that perhaps helped him see the lighter side of life. Yet, even for my father, the moments of laughter were rare.

Our survival depended on reaching the Soviet-occupied eastern part of Poland. My family believed that the Soviets did not harbor the Nazis' hatred of the Jews and would not bomb innocent civilians. So a decision was made to keep pushing east, day and night, in all kinds of weather. The roads were less congested at night, so we were able to cover greater distances. But traveling at night was dangerous. We heard there were gangs of bandits roaming the backcountry roads, robbing the refugees. Also, traveling at night proved to be difficult without the sun to guide us in the right direction.

Most people in our group, but especially the ones walking beside the wagon, were always extremely tired. Often, bad weather made our situation worse. The rains turned the dirt roads into mud, and the wheels of our heavy wagon sank deep into the mud. At times like that, my parents, aunts, uncles, and cousins, their feet in the mud, their fingers sticking out of torn gloves, got behind the wagon and pushed to help the tired horse. The cold, the wet, the fatigue, the hard work—and the anxiety—were bad for our health. It wasn't only the Germans we feared; we were getting sick. I heard coughing all the time.

One night in October, Frydzia and I were fast asleep in the chilly, open-air wagon. Cousin Bella and her two little daughters, Frydzia (the same name as my sister) and Syma, were also asleep. The others were walking slowly. We were awakened by a strange voice coming from nowhere. The night was dark—no moonlight. It was damp; it felt like being swallowed up in a thick fog. The air was calm. Everything seemed still, except for the voice. Soon, the words got louder, but we couldn't make out their meaning.

All at once, we glimpsed a figure emerging from the darkness. He continued advancing toward us, all the time shouting and waving his hands. Even in the darkness, as he drew closer, he seemed different from the men in my family. In the stillness of the night, his voice was resonant with deep, echoing sounds. He approached the wagon, and we noticed he had no luggage. He was running with nothing in his hands—so strange in those days of war and refugees. He appeared larger and taller than the men in our family. Even stranger were the clothes he wore. They were all white. Looking out of the wagon and staring at the vision, I thought to myself, *Surely, this has to be what God looks like.*

He drew still nearer, and now he appeared to be Jewish, with a beard like my uncles. Then we heard his voice, clearly, in Yiddish. "Jews, Jews, where are you going? Go back!" he called out to us. "You are heading straight to the Germans."

The stranger kept running. Soon, he disappeared from view. On the narrow, muddy road, it was extremely difficult to turn the wagon around. Even for the men in my family, it was a real struggle.

We never saw the stranger again. He came from nowhere and disappeared into nowhere, yet he wasn't a dream. That we all knew for sure. We spoke of him often. Members of my family believed that the white clothing he wore was a white *talith*, the Jewish prayer shawl. We remembered him in good times and in bad times, especially when we needed another miracle.

7
Warm Welcome

We had been on the road nearly two months. The weather was changing. The nights were cold. The leaves were turning color and clinging to the branches with their last breath of life. We were getting very skinny for lack of food. My aunts, who were rather plump before the outbreak of war, were now becoming slim. But Mama, who was slim before the war, was getting really skinny. Everyone talked nonstop about the Soviets. "How close are we? Will the Nazis catch up with us before we reach the Soviets?"

One day, as our poor horse pushed on ever so slowly, we heard extraordinary sounds coming from what seemed a great distance. Then, just around the corner, we stumbled upon the entire Soviet armed forces. That's how it seemed to me, at any rate. They were everywhere—artillery, armored vehicles, and soldiers on foot. We couldn't see anything past the mighty force. For us, this was the greatest miracle of all. We were exhausted, but we were rejoicing. My pious relatives, in their bedraggled, old prayer shawls, intoned special prayers. They believed we had been delivered from evil. Uncle Benjamin, my youngest uncle—I called him Uncle Beno—believed that it was God who had guided us all the way. Most likely, we managed to evade the Germans by traveling through tiny hamlets and villages. We looked for small, out-of-the-way dirt roads accessible to horse and wagon. In the two months on the road, we barely covered two hundred miles, whereas the Germans, seizing the major roads, overran virtually all of Poland in two to three weeks.

I remember the Soviet soldiers in faded green uniforms, red five-pointed stars attached to the fronts of the peaked caps. They wore high-collared shirts, with wide leather belts fastened tightly around the waist. Below the cinched belts, the shirts flared out as they did on Cossacks ready to perform a native dance. I liked those uniforms, and I liked the soldiers. They were good to us; they gave us bread. Bread was what we liked and had missed most of all.

The soldiers greeted us in Russian. I understood some of the words; I thought the language very similar to Polish. Some of the soldiers, recognizing—thanks to my bearded uncles—that we were Jewish, spoke to us in Yiddish. Unlike the unpleasant Polish soldiers, the Russians were a godsend.

Almost immediately, the family decided to stay put. We all felt safe with the Soviets. The coachman unloaded our bundles. I felt especially sad saying good-bye to our dear, old horse. It was the horse, our best friend, that had really delivered us from evil. The coachman prepared for the long journey back home, packing up the many gold coins our family had given him—Polish money was worthless—for having gotten us far from the dreaded Nazis.

We reached a small town called Brzuchowice. Before the outbreak of war, Brzuchowice was part of Poland. After September 17, 1939, Poland no longer existed as an independent and free country. It was divided between Nazi Germany and the Soviet Union. Our extended family settled in Brzuchowice in what had become, in an instant, the Ukraine Soviet Socialist

Republic. My parents, my sister, and I said good-bye to the rest of the family and pushed farther east. I've no idea why Papa decided to move on. Maybe he felt we had not put enough distance between us and the Nazis. Maybe the family needed some separation. The last two months had put a tremendous strain on the familial relationship.

8
Summer Villa

I have no recollection of finally arriving in Lwow (present-day Lviv), the largest city in that part of Ukraine, that had also become the Ukraine Soviet Socialist Republic. It was November or early December. The shooting and bombing were over, but the consequences of war remained visible, and the human suffering continued. People were homeless; they appeared sad and discouraged, roaming the streets aimlessly, looking for shelter and food.

The streets were covered in snow; it was cold. We were homeless in the dead of winter. As always, I believed that Mama and Papa would make everything right. I believed in my parents, and in spite of all that had happened, I still believed in God. All my life, I heard the phrase "God will provide." I felt safe that, between my parents and God, everything would turn out right in time.

During the day, Mama and Papa ran around the city looking for lodging. Frydzia and I tried to stay warm in the large railway station among hundreds of refugees. Many nights, we slept on the floor of the station.

One afternoon, our parents returned to the station with wonderful news. They had found a room with a bed. They looked so happy, so radiant. Papa literally scooped Frydzia and me off the floor. "We're leaving the station," he said. "We're going to our new home." Mama and Papa grabbed us and the bundles, and we were off.

Our new home was a room in the rear of a vacation house on the outskirts of Lwow. It was a beautiful villa with large windows. There were gardens in the front and rear with benches and birdbaths, now all covered in snow. But the summer villa had no heating other than the big, wood-burning stone fireplace in the front parlor.

We shared the villa with a man in his fifties and his son, perhaps in his twenties or thirties. They had the use of the front parlor, the kitchen, and the bathroom. We were allowed to use the bathroom most of the time and the kitchen only occasionally. Both father and son did not like us very much. I recall overhearing anti-Semitic remarks about us coming from the front room. They cooked pork. The unfamiliar smells from the kitchen drifted into our room. We had very little food, but eating pork seemed strange to me. I couldn't imagine eating it. Later in the war, I would have been happy to eat pork or any food, even food I disliked before the war.

Our room was cold, but the down quilt we had brought from home was a godsend. Frydzia and I tried to keep warm under the quilt while Mama and Papa were out looking for food. For them, finding food was a daily, ongoing preoccupation.

9
Warm Oven

The Jewish community in Lwow was another godsend for us. They welcomed us with open arms, as if we were family. They were generous in spirit. Often, we sat with total strangers at their dinner tables. They didn't have a lot of food—no one did in those difficult times—but they did offer us their favorite seats near a warm oven and a glass of hot tea (a glass of hot tea was a hot oven for the hands).

I recall one particularly warm home with a hot oven. Mama found some flour and a little sugar somewhere. The family offered to let her use their oven to bake her delicious little round buns with sugar sprinkled on top. I will never forget those buns—warm and light like a feather and oh so sweet. Before the war, Mama baked the most wonderful cakes, cookies, and the traditional twisted challahs for the Sabbath. Yet the simple little buns she baked in someone else's home were the best I ever tasted. Baking sweet buns in other peoples' homes ... that spelled love to me, for Mama was never one for many words. It was the daily sacrifices; it's what she *did* that mattered. It came from her heart. But always, I saw her love in her eyes.

I have good memories of the Jewish people of Lwow. We didn't stay long in Lwow, only three or four months. It was lucky for us that we were like nomads, always on the move, because that saved our lives. Unfortunately, no one could foresee the tragic end to the Jewish people of Lwow.

Germany declared war on the Soviet Union on June 22, 1941. The whole Jewish community of Lwow was wiped out shortly thereafter by the Nazis—aided by the Ukrainians.

10
Frosty Window

The winter of 1939/40 was not a good winter at all. Life under the Soviet occupation was difficult in so many ways. Firewood, coal, or fuel of any kind was hard to come by. People stole sections of wooden fences to stay warm, even if just for a few days. For my family, finding food was the main preoccupation and a constant struggle. The extreme cold made our lives even more difficult. We kept hearing that this was the coldest winter on record. We were losing weight for lack of food and extremely cold temperatures.

Our single room in the summer villa was unheated, and it was as cold inside as outside. Even indoors, we wore everything we owned—coats, scarves, and hats. Outside, everything was covered in a blanket of snow, and sidewalks were sheets of ice.

Still, I loved the beautiful winter scene, and I loved to play in the snow. I was able to forget our precarious living conditions when experiencing the beautiful winter wonderland. It brought joy to my heart.

Our room, on the other hand, was no cause for joy. Sometimes, a gust of wind blew the snowdrifts right through the broken window frames into our room, forming snowdrifts on the inside of the windowsills. The entire window was perpetually encased in frost. We could no longer see out.

Frydzia and I had no toys, no books, no friends to play with. But we had our frosty window. I believed there was something magical about the leaves and flowers that seemed etched into the window glass.

With our fingernails, we drew the outlines of the lovely designs formed by the frost. We treasured the frosty window. It was better than a doll, a game, or any toy because it was alive and dynamic, always changing. I felt as if I could communicate with the window. It always responded by creating new images. Sometimes, we used the frosty window to write numbers and letters of the alphabet. Sometimes, we pressed our hands with fingers extended against the frozen glass, which resulted in interesting hand impressions. Frydzia would joyfully call out, "Oh look. My hand is bigger and better than yours."

We discovered that the frosty window had many possibilities. Very soon, we learned that blowing air out of our mouths created a circle of clear window glass. I fantasized that, during the night, Mr. Frost, with his magic brush, would transform the clear circle into the most beautiful designs just to amuse us the next morning.

The frosty window was an escape from our dreary living conditions. I wanted to remain in the frosty window fantasyland and not be reminded of our fragile existence.

11
A Rabbi's Talith

In addition to the daily struggle to find food, my mother and father disagreed on many issues. Their loud "discussions" were about the possibility of returning home. We heard nothing from our family back home on the "other" side, in the Nazi-occupied parts of Poland. Perhaps their mail was being censored and couldn't get through to us.

Still, Mama insisted we go back, even if it meant going back to the Nazis. She had left behind four sisters and brothers, nieces, nephews, and cousins, and she missed them terribly. I think she didn't understand that life as we remembered it before September 1 was gone forever. No one did. Even my father didn't have a clue. But he remained steadfast in his belief that one should never be in the presence of a uniformed Nazi soldier, especially not Jewish people. He understood that such a toxic form of anti-Semitism could kill you in the end. He took it seriously. He repeated his views frequently. And history proved him right.

One day, I overheard another "discussion." For me, it was scarier than ever. Papa was telling my mother very emphatically that he would not accompany her if she insisted on going back to Nazi-occupied Poland, and under no circumstances would he allow her to take the children. I didn't care about the cold or hunger. I didn't care whether we stayed or went back. I just wanted to keep my parents and Frydzia—all four of us—together. This discussion sounded to me like the end of everything. It seemed like the end of our family and was too awful even to contemplate. But days and weeks passed, and I didn't hear another word about going back. Our room was quiet at last. I was happier.

~

There was a knock on our door one cold night. In walked the rabbi from our town! Mama and Papa were surprised, to say the least, to see him. He too was so far from home. I listened, even though I was repeatedly told not to eavesdrop on adult conversation; there was nothing else for me to do. The rabbi's appearance had changed since we saw him last in our town's old synagogue at Sabbath services. He seemed dispirited and somewhat disheveled. He looked so sad. I didn't like seeing my rabbi in such bad shape.

Then I overheard him say that he missed his wife and his five children so terribly that he needed to be with them, even if it meant going back to the Nazis. He wanted to know if my parents ever considered going back. Papa said he understood the rabbi's need to be reunited with his family, but going back was not an option for our family.

"If we can help it," Papa told the rabbi, "we will not lay eyes on a Nazi uniform."

Then the rabbi reached into his satchel and pulled out a talith, his prayer shawl, and handed it to my father. "I'm leaving my talith with you for safekeeping," he said. "I know that you will take good care of it." And Papa promised he would.

I didn't understand why the rabbi would leave his talith with my father. After all, Papa already had his own talith. Besides, it was unthinkable for any pious Jew—especially a rabbi—to leave behind a talith! I have long wondered since then if the rabbi had a premonition that he, his family, and the talith would not survive. Indeed, the rabbi and all his family perished in the Holocaust, but the prayer shawl survived intact, as Papa had promised.

To this day, we treasure the talith. Several of Papa's great-grandchildren celebrated their bar mitzvahs draped in the rabbi's old talith.

But that was a long way off. And in that desperate winter of 1939/40, no one could have foreseen all that still awaited us.

12
White Stockings

One day, Mama told Frydzia and me to dress nicely. We didn't have a whole wardrobe to choose from, just the same old coats, hats, and scarves. I did have a pair of white stockings. I wore those.

Mama didn't tell us where she was taking us, and Papa wasn't around to voice his objections to Mama's plans for the day. I began to worry. I understood that anything out of the ordinary could unravel our lives even more. My mother walked quickly. She seemed full of angry determination. Frydzia and I ran, trying to keep up with her. Finally, she said she was taking us to school. She didn't say anything else.

Only when we got there did I understand that it was no ordinary school. The building itself was enormous, part of a convent, attached to a church with a tall spire and a cross on top.

As we climbed a steep flight of stairs, I couldn't help thinking how it was strange for someone like my mother—a

Jewish Orthodox woman—even to contemplate enrolling us in anything other than a Jewish or public school.

The contrast between the bright, snow-covered streets and the dark interior of the wood-paneled corridor inside the building was almost blinding. Mama instructed us to sit on a bench along the wall. As my eyesight adjusted to the darkness, the place didn't seem so dark after all. Mama approached a nun who was dressed in black from head to toe. I saw her speaking to the nun but couldn't make out the words. I needed desperately to know what was being said. Was my mother pleading with the nun to take us in? Would we be going to live there? The thought was terrifying, and the terror—the stress of not knowing what was going on—affected me physically. I felt ill and was afraid of getting sick onto the highly polished floors. As I always did at times like that, I willed myself to remain very still.

Minutes later, I observed a movement of uniforms inching forward in our direction. They were boys and girls my age, walking in pairs, holding hands, and attentively listening to the instructions given by another nun. I was amazed to see so many children not making a sound. It was unsettling. I had never witnessed such perfect behavior before.

From a distance, I saw the nun and my mother terminating their conversation. Mama turned. Without another word, she took us by our hands and rushed us out of the convent. Then she explained that the school would not enroll Jewish children. "But don't worry," she said. "Soon, I'll find another school for you."

I didn't worry. In fact, I was overjoyed; I felt as if I had just discovered something wonderful. I was almost flying in the air as we descended the steep flight of stairs. The air felt chilly but so refreshing.

13
A Knock on the Door

Finally, the long winter was over. We grew tired of the constant struggle to fill our stomachs, to stay warm with only a candle for the long, dark nights.

After much debate, Mama and Papa finally decided what direction our lives were to take next. They discussed the possibility of departing from Lwow. They were throwing ideas at each other, frequently arguing. Their various plans ran the entire gamut of survival possibilities. Mama, as always, nagged about returning home to Nazi-occupied Poland. Papa remained adamant against going back. To this day, I am in awe of his strength and determination to resist Mama's demands. Had he given in, none of us would have survived.

I tried to stay out of their way, make myself almost invisible, and remain oblivious to everything pertaining to our difficulties. I didn't want to hear about the war and the struggle to survive. I needed to be left out of life's harsh realities.

I sensed rather than knew that we were living a hand-to-mouth existence that depended on intelligence, common sense, and gumption. Money held no sustained value in the Soviet economy at that time. Tradable goods were the real currency; they were the assets that counted, and I was somehow aware that my parents—like everyone else—often struggled to find a way to survive. Somehow, they managed to keep us all alive.

That spring of 1940 brought with it a sense of awakening. Snows began to melt. Even tiny purple and yellow flowers made their appearance from under the melting snows. The short, dark days of winter gave way to brighter days, and occasional rays of sunshine began to peek through the breaks in the overcast skies.

On our windowpane, the frozen leaves and flowers melted away. We opened the window for the first time in months and let the spring air in. And for the first time in months, Frydzia and I ventured out. It was glorious to breathe the fragrant, moist air and to feel the wet snow on my hands and face. I was so happy. I saw and felt the beauty in nature and needed to be a part of it.

One day, our parents packed up our meager belongings, and we took to the road again. We went back to Brzuchowice, a small town—particularly compared to Lwow—surrounded by deep forests and meadows for cattle grazing. It was only about fifty miles from Lwow and, of course, was where many in our extended family had decided to stay. We had been able to keep in touch with them during the long winter months because Brzuchowice was part of the Soviet-occupied Poland as well.

Mama and Papa agreed that being reunited with family would ease the struggle to survive in harsh conditions—if for no other reason than our need for the emotional connection.

The reunion was warm and happy. My aunts and cousins cried openly, and some of the uncles had to work hard to conceal their emotions. There was tiny Tante Esther with her perpetually scarf-covered head. I guess she had left her sheitel at home when we all ran away. Uncle Benjamin—the older Benjamin—Esther's husband, grinned from ear to ear. Cousin

Bella showed off her brand-new four-month-old baby, Lily. But the happiest moment for me was when I ran into the open arms of Tante Bronia. Seeing us again, Uncle Beno, Bronia's husband, burst into tears and smiled with happiness. At last we were together, all fourteen of us—fifteen with the baby!—and life was going be good again.

Our family members lived in hunters' cabins in the woods. They made room for us in one of them. In those days, accommodating friends or family was hardly ever a problem. We slept wherever we could stretch out—on the floor, on wooden benches, wherever. A couple of cots were reserved for the most senior members of the family—namely, Tante Esther and her husband, Uncle Benjamin.

In the center of the cabin stood a wood-burning potbelly stove made of iron. The delightful crackling sound of wood burning in the stove was music to our ears, especially after enduring our cold room during the long winter in Lwow. The stove was also the focal point for socializing. Uncles and cousins stretched out their hands, almost touching the stove in an attempt to keep warm and dry but really keeping warm through heated discussions.

Politics was high on the list of topics. I learned a lot from eavesdropping on those conversations. But hearing that Hitler had invaded Holland, Belgium, and then France was especially frightening to me. From those conversations, I surmised that no one could stop Hitler and that the war was never going to end, and we would never go back home.

Of course, the stove was mainly for cooking an occasional soup or boiling water for tea. Sometimes, we made our own potato chips. We peeled potatoes, cut them into very thin round or oval slices, sprinkled them with salt, and threw them on top of the hot stove. They were probably the best potato chips I had ever eaten.

Frydzia and I and our two little cousins Syma and Frydzia (both Frydzias were named after Frymet, the same grandmother) played with their brand-new baby sister, Lily. For us, she was like a little toy. We also played in the woods, mostly hide-and-seek. We helped my mother and our aunts plant potato peels that would soon yield a real crop of potatoes—a promise of keeping hunger at bay the entire summer.

The meadows were fragrant with flowers. I ran around picking more flowers than I could possibly carry in my arms. I believe that, as young as I was, I understood the language of flowers even then. For the first time in many months, life seemed more normal, especially for us children.

But all was not well, especially for the adults in our family.

There were disquieting rumors going around. It was said that some people, especially young, single men, were disappearing, being arrested in the middle of the night by the Soviets and shipped off to distant Siberian camps (gulags), never to be heard from again.

We were a large family with young children—that made us feel secure. After all, the Soviets did not need young children in their camps. Or so we thought until one night when our false sense of security was shattered. Heavy pounding on the door and harsh voices ordering us in Russian to open up awoke all of us. What happened that night changed our lives forever. It also saved us all.

14
Deportation

In June 1940, the war took a new turn. Italy joined Germany to form the Axis powers, and the Soviet Union forcibly annexed the Baltic states—Estonia, Latvia, and Lithuania—deporting thousands of people to camps around the Soviet Union run by the NKVD (also known as the KGB), the dreaded secret police. Among other consequences, this meant that Brzuchowice was now situated just over the easternmost border of the Third Reich.

It was 4:00 a.m. when we heard the pounding. Papa answered the door. Two Soviet soldiers, rifles at their sides, confronted him. Suddenly, everyone in the hut was awake. There were just two soldiers, but their presence was overpowering. They seemed to take up the entire space around us. In the hut next door, I heard familiar voices and the baby crying. There were soldiers with rifles there too.

"Get ready," the lead soldier ordered us in a loud, menacing voice. "You have half an hour to gather up your things. Not too much!"

"Where are you taking us?" Papa asked.

"Just get ready. No questions!"

"But we need to know what to pack," Papa persisted.

"Stop speaking!" the soldier screamed.

Papa hung his head and turned to us. "Dress quickly," he said quietly. "Wear as much as you can—one dress on top of the other. We cannot pack too much. We must get ready to leave."

My mother's quiet resignation was all too familiar to me. But what had happened to my father? He seemed to have changed. This forlorn, submissive Papa was something new and different, and it didn't feel right. I was almost seven, and my father was thirty-eight. He was our family's strength and seemed to me a giant in so many ways. He was dependable, and he would protect us always. I had never witnessed anyone addressing him in such a threatening manner, and I certainly had never imagined seeing him walk away so defeated. My father was powerless and submissive to these intruders. It was all a new reality, one I was too young to understand. But instinctively, I knew that my world was made less secure because of my father's new vulnerability.

I grabbed Papa's arm, tugging at his sleeve, wanting desperately to shake him back to being my old, dependable Papa. But I too felt defeated, and I began wailing like a wounded animal.

"You must stop crying immediately," Papa said. Papa's stern voice brought back to mind the old Papa. It felt better, familiar. Later, I would learn that some of the relatives had been frightened by my outburst. They believed that my crying had endangered all our lives. But I couldn't help it.

Then I began thinking about Tante Bronia. They lived not too far from us. The awful soldiers were taking us away, and I would never see my favorite aunt again. I would never hear the wonderful stories she told. I could not bear to be separated from

Tante Bronia; the very thought felt like a choking sensation, and I cried even harder.

"What about Tante Bronia and Uncle Beno?" I asked. "Are they coming with us?"

"What's that you said?" the soldier asked. "Who are they? Where do they live?" And I told him.

Then I looked up at Mama and Papa, and what I saw in their eyes was such sadness and disappointment. I did not understand until much later what I had done. I had given away the whereabouts of my aunt and uncle—I had made it easy for the Soviets to round them up for deportation.

At daybreak, with the rest of the family from the hut next door, we were marched to the railway station. We walked quietly. I held Papa's hand tightly. Mama and Frydzia walked hand in hand. Papa kept looking at the armed soldiers. Maybe he hoped for an explanation, but I knew he didn't dare to speak up again. The soldiers offered no explanation.

The sun was breaking through the overcast sky as we arrived at the station. Groups of people crowded the length of the platform along the railroad tracks, no train in sight. Yet many more soldiers armed with rifles were patrolling the newly arrived people at the station. I couldn't understand where all these people came from, just standing at the rails.

Many were families like ours, also with young children. Some were young, single people, standing as if in a trance. As the crowd grew, the scene became chaotic—more and more people, more and more armed guards. Mama, seated on the floor next to our bundles, seemed in a state of shock and exhaustion. Her chin in her hand, she seemed to be crying. I looked around. Many people were crying. No one had real luggage, hardly any suitcases, just things thrown together into sheets or blankets, just as we had done.

Suddenly, out of nowhere, in the middle of the teeming humanity, I spotted Tante Bronia and Uncle Beno. I felt proud of myself that I had given the right address to the soldiers because now they were here with us again.

"Tante Bronia!" I choked on the name. "I'm so happy you are here with us. I thought I would never see you again." My aunt held me in her arms, lovingly stroking my face.

"We searched for you all over," she said. "But everything will be fine now that we are all together." I don't recall ever feeling happier than at that moment when I spotted my aunt and uncle at the crowded station.

The train arrived at last, only this was no ordinary train— brown, wooden boxcars as far as the eye could see. It was the length of the entire station. At the center of each car, heavy, metal sliding doors were simultaneously unbolted by guards with rifles hanging from their shoulders. The clanking sounds were disturbing. The guards began herding us into the cavernous space.

Within moments, the car we were ushered into with our extended family was filled to capacity. Every inch of space was taken up. My immediate family settled near the door. Leaning out the door, I could see along the entire platform as people struggled to climb into the cars. It was difficult; the opening was high—too high for an average person to reach. The guards propped slanted boards up against the edge of the cars to make a bridge for the old and disabled, helping many of them up into the boxcar.

There were two windows in the boxcar, one on each side of the door and high up near the ceiling—like high, narrow slits staring out at the world. Propped up under each window hung a wooden board. It looked like a small bunk bed without a mattress, not even a straw mat. If you managed to climb up there, you could see out. It was a bunk bed with a view—the only way to see out during the long journey ahead. Sometimes, Frydzia and I climbed up there—but only for a short stay. It was the most desirable space of all. It was dry and warm, and it was the best place to escape from the people below.

Almost immediately, everyone tried to carve out space for themselves and their own families. My parents did the same. Some people seemed overcome with exhaustion, oblivious—or simply indifferent—to anything going on around them. Some slept curled up in a fetal position, for there was no way to stretch out.

Women cradled their cranky and tired children in their arms. The children were allowed to lie down completely stretched out during the long journey. Maybe that was an unspoken rule. Sometimes, very young children stretched their entire bodies on top of their own parents' legs. Maybe they derived from this an extra bit of security in those terribly insecure times. I slept on Mama's or Papa's legs sometimes too. Most adults slept sitting up.

Some people behaved badly. Almost everyone grew territorial—perhaps normal in crowded places where space is important and where some locations are better than others. Maybe the terrible circumstances brought out the worst in people. Yet those same terrible circumstances also brought out the best. I saw kindness. I saw people sharing food with strangers. I saw strangers comforting other people's children, even making funny faces to amuse them or singing songs with them.

Before long, the doors were bolted shut. Again, the sound of steel clanking against steel throughout the whole length of the train was disturbing. I was overcome with fear of that awful sound. I heard the other children crying too. With the doors shut, we could not see out. We also couldn't see much inside the car. We sat in semidarkness. The two narrow windows high up near the ceiling were like two eyes that shed a little light into the cavernous interior.

I made myself very small and squeezed between Mama and Papa, all the time envying Frydzia holding Mama so tightly. I needed to hold them all, but I wasn't big enough to embrace them fully.

People began to talk. "Where are they taking us? What will they do with us?" No one knew, but everyone could speculate. "If the Soviets don't like you for political, religious, or social views, I hear they ship you off to Siberia," said one man, and this view was much discussed and argued. Most people were in agreement on one thing, however—that whatever our final destination, we were never going home again. More than anything in the whole world, I wanted to go home.

"Please, God," I prayed, "I will be so good, if only you take us back home." Sometimes, I closed my eyes very tight and fantasized that the train was turning around and that soon we would be home. Almost immediately, I learned that prayers didn't always work—maybe sometimes, but not always.

The train sped on, the wheels rotating faster and faster. It had been many hours since we were taken out of our hut. Naturally, our need to use a toilet had become urgent. The "bathroom" was a huge and deep bucket filled with disinfectant, surrounded by a heavy canvas sheet. It was located in the center of the car, and it smelled terrible from the toxic disinfectant.

But as uncomfortable as all this was, the uncertainties in our lives and the deprivations created a situation beyond discomfort. We had nothing to eat, and we had nothing to drink for hours, not since we were taken out of our hut. We were locked in, completely shut off from the rest of the world in a dark and claustrophobic environment. We had no way of knowing if or when the train would make a stop, if we would get food or water. We had no contact with our guards or with anyone who could tell us what was happening or what to expect. Where we were going?

I was only a child, and having my parents there made it a little better. When I cried, they were reassuring; they promised food soon, and I believed it. I clung to them. They gave me the secure feeling I needed. What they and the other adults felt on the long journey is hard to imagine.

15
Long Journey East

Only the guards knew our destination, but they did not communicate with us at all. Locked in our tightly packed containers, we felt the train's speed. The steady, rocking motion and the sound of the wheels against the rails were strangely soothing. The windows allowed slits of daylight into the darkness of the car, and tiny rays of sunshine peeked through the cracks in the doorframe and along the sides of the car. People were glued to those openings, trying to see out.

It was hot that June of our deportation. The sun beat down on us. It was stuffy—hardly any air—and people wiped sweat off their faces with crumpled, soiled handkerchiefs.

In the sweltering heat and confinement of the cattle car, the mood kept changing.

The sound of loud words exploded like thunder in the sky as people fought over inches of space.

"This is my spot!"

"No, it's not! You don't own the spot; you don't own anything."

Then there would be a dispirited quiet, and the mood would retreat into silence.

Most people sat on the floor, tired and resigned to the uncertainties in their lives. Some seemed asleep, rolled into a small, human ball.

I hated being confined in that tight space. I hated the smell of sweat, hated people sitting too close to me. I felt miserable and confused. A few short months earlier, we were still home. My life was normal then, sheltered from anything resembling this ugly side of life. I wanted to be home again. I believed Mama and Papa could make this happen.

"Papa, when can we go home? Please, I want to see my friends, I want to go home. Please!" I cried and I nagged, and they always promised—soon.

"Soon, we will go home, and you'll play with your friends."

And I believed them; their small lies made me feel better. I clung to my parents. I wanted to stay in their arms. This was my way of escaping the imprisonment of my surroundings.

We had traveled some two or three hours when we felt the train slowing down, the wheels rotating more slowly, the car vibrating less vigorously. Since we couldn't see out, it was these minute changes that provided a sense of what was happening. We hoped for a train stop. We needed food and water desperately. We wished for some contact with our jailers, which was better than no contact at all.

Finally, the train came to a stop. Again, we heard the loud and disturbing sound of metal doors being unbolted. Then there was food. In front of the opened door stood an enormous metal kettle filled to the top with something resembling a thick soup or porridge. It was ladled out into large, tin cups along with some sticky brown bread. One by one, we were instructed to reach out for the soup near the door. No one could get a double portion, as the tin cups were accounted for—one per "passenger." We were told to finish the soup and keep the cups for future "meals." I don't recall anything tasting as good as the porridge of that day. We ate our dinner to the sound of metal doors being bolted again.

As the days passed, it became clear we were heading east. We came first into Ukraine, with its rich, fertile soil, lush meadows, and orchards. Some peasants stood near the tracks, holding their farming equipment and waving to us, bidding us, "Good-bye and good riddance." Jews were not welcome in that part of the world.

The beautiful countryside could only be seen while sitting up high on the wooden board under the sliver of the narrow window. People fought over that space. It was literally portioned out, with someone always keeping track if others used it too often or stayed up there too long.

In time, we came into Russia proper, traveling along the great river Volga, the largest river in the European part of Soviet Russia. The doors were unbolted again as we approached the crossing of the river. We were amazed at the enormous expanse of water. It was impossible to see the other bank of the river. Russian people revere this great river. It brings forth powerful emotions. For them, it is mother love, and they call it Volga Matushka in Russian—Mother Volga.

The guards never disclosed our destination. "When do we eat?" and "Where are you taking us?"—those were the two most frequently asked questions on all our minds. The guards brought us food—not much but enough to keep us from starving. Sometimes, they made jokes as they ladled the soup from the deep bucket. "You'll eat roast chicken and fried potatoes for supper tonight!" they would say. The Soviet guards did not hate us for being Jewish as the Nazis did back home in Poland, but they made sure we followed orders. We were not allowed to step out of the train when the doors were unbolted at station stops, and they always counted the number of people before bolting the doors shut again.

As the days became weeks, it grew obvious that we were heading toward Siberia. I have no recollection when we first discovered our true destination. The relationship between the guards and us grew more relaxed. As we reached the enormous forested land of Siberia, the guards no longer feared that we would run away. Where could we run in that vast land?

16
End of Journey

The journey lasted six weeks and ended in Krasnoyarsk, one of the largest Siberian cities. We were ordered to disembark from the cattle train. As we stepped down into the expansive station, I noted the name in huge Cyrillic letters high up near the vaulted ceiling. I have no recollection of getting into a horse-drawn wagon with my family. But I do remember the stillness and the peaceful beauty of the forest, interrupted only by the rhythmic sound of horses' hooves on the soft, dirt road.

Days later and many miles to the north, we were dropped off in our new "home," the Siberian camp that nobody ever escapes from. I glanced around and saw small and large tree-log barracks freshly constructed, probably in great haste to receive us—the new inmates of a vast Siberian territory. Small chunks of downed trees were scattered on the soft ground, while pine needles, sawdust, and wood chips made a cushiony path leading to the entrance of the barracks. I loved the pine trees, thick shrubs, and the flowers that seemed to grow taller than I was.

I bent down and squeezed my hands through the soft ground cover and brought a handful to my face. I closed my eyes and breathed deeply the scent of my new surroundings. The pungent scent of freshly cut trees was palpable, and the fragrance was intoxicating. The gentle Siberian sun caressed my face. It felt good. I clung to the cart horse; his warmth warmed me too.

It was July 1940. A few days earlier was my birthday. I had turned seven, but I felt old—as if my soul was old. The ugly barracks—stark, odd, and out of place—would be my home for the rest of my life. How could this be? Only the beauty of the forest surrounding the camp lent some charm to the ugliness of the brand-new construction.

We were not fenced in. There were no barbed wires, no bars on windows. Yet we were imprisoned as surely as any criminals could ever be. With the exception of a tiny settlement outpost many miles away, there was nothing but wooded wilderness in every direction. There was no point in running; there was nowhere to run, nothing to run to.

"*Previcnete ele podokhnete,*" our guards told us—right from the beginning. This rhyming phrase had a simple meaning, although its language was somewhat unpleasant: "You'll get used to it, or you'll die." As they would also explain, "You don't need guards; nature is your guard."

17
Siberian Summer

If one were to get used to life in Siberia, summer was probably the best time of the year. But summers were short, lasting only from June through the end of August. During the summer months, the woods were full of edible vegetation—grass that tasted sour and wild onions and wild seeds that grew in abundance. Frequently, we dug out all sorts of roots that grew in the clearing. It was hard labor. All of us searched for edible stuff, even we the little children.

Best were the mushrooms and berries that grew deep in the forest. We ate the berries raw. But the soup that my mother made from mushrooms and wild onions and seeds remains in the deepest recesses of my consciousness as the most delicious food I have ever eaten. Of course, I have eaten better-tasting food since those long-gone days, but never have I eaten food that satisfied so well.

There was a downside to picking berries. The forest and the clearing were also home to the largest and most vicious mosquitoes in the world. Only smoke and fire kept them away. They were especially cruel to the children. For me, berry picking represented a personal fight with the mosquitoes. I believed that they were greedy animals unwilling to share the abundance of the forest. My perseverance, however, usually resulted in mosquito stings that swelled my face almost beyond recognition.

The banks of the river Yenisey were our playground. In the early summer, I enjoyed watching the rushing waters, swollen from melted snows, flooding the grassy shores. It was not unusual to walk on solidly packed snow early in the morning and then find a water hole filled with freezing snowmelt on the route home from school in the afternoon. Frydzia and I learned early on how to navigate these brand-new bodies of water. You walked around them very, very carefully.

There was a huge boulder that I loved to sit on, from which I could observe the life on the river. I loved to watch tree logs floating down the river and men standing on top of them, holding long wooden poles and gently "steering" the logs away from the shore. Often, I fantasized that I could hold on to a log and float gently away to some distant and mysterious land.

But most amusing of all were the vibrant birds flying low in search of little ripples in the water that were a sign of fish just below the surface. They all seemed to be traveling in the same direction, all in perfect harmony, a splendid concert in nature that never ceased to amaze me.

One day, while sitting on top of my favorite rock, dangling my legs and feeling rather happy, one of my sandals fell into the water. With horror and fascination, I watched the river take away my sandal. How could I go home without my sandal? What would Mama say? This was my only pair of sandals and my only pair of summer shoes. Young as I was, I understood that anything lost in Siberia could not be replaced. Instinctively, I reached for the clasp in my hair. What if I lost it? How would my hair stay in place? I used to think about it constantly, almost obsessively. Then I remembered the lost sandal. How would I explain to Mama what had happened? Crying, I ran home, my left foot inside the sandal, my right foot in the wet soil and prickly shrubs. Mama didn't say much as she stared down at my feet. She just stood there in bewildered silence. I remember to this day that nothing she had ever said to me sounded as loud as the silence over the lost sandal.

If summers had their charm, the Siberian winters were harsh beyond anything we had ever experienced before. Quilted outerwear, fur, and animal skins were best for enduring the long and harsh winters. Ordinary boots did not protect feet from frostbite. The best boots, called valenky, were made of heavy, pressed felt, molded and shaped like boots and kept the feet warm. They were housing for the feet.

But we did not own *valenky* or animal skins. Only the guards and some native Siberians did. We had to improvise. When I outgrew my only pair of winter shoes, Papa cut open the front parts, separating them from the soles, so I could wrap my open toes in rags and paper. Still, both my feet got frostbitten that first winter. I recall Mama rubbing snow on my bare feet in a desperate effort to restore blood circulation to my toes. I screamed from intense pain as my feet began to defrost.

Winter lasted nine to ten months of the year. The snow began to fall in September, sometimes for weeks on end. The howling winds blew from the Arctic north, piling snow under our little window, sometimes blocking the heavy wooden door from the outside. It was hard to find food. Nothing grew anymore. Everything was covered in a blanket of snow.

We depended on the daily bowl of cooked barley or porridge with a heavy layer of fish oil on top. The hot cereal was portioned out in the camp communal kitchen. Frydzia and I loved the cereal but hated the fish oil. Mama was strict about it.

"You will eat it as served. It's good for you. It will keep you full and keep hunger away," she was quick to point out.

On rare occasions, we were given frozen milk shaped like a brick of ice. Papa would smash it with a large rock, and we chewed the pieces of splintered, frozen milk; it was quite wonderful, a real treat.

Like animals in the woods, we grew hungrier and skinnier. But unlike the animals in the woods, we could not dig holes and wait out the winter underground.

∽

People died, and there were funerals in Siberia. I remember one funeral; it is fixed firmly in my memory. I had gone to play with a friend in another barracks. It was one of the largest barracks, with dozens of bunk beds lining both sides of the room. I was happy that my friend and I were going to pick flowers and explore the outdoors. Instead of picking flowers, I found my friend alone, sitting on the floor next to a bunk bed where her mother lay very still, seemingly asleep. Yet I knew she was dead. I remembered people "asleep" like that—the day of the bombing.

I'm not sure my friend knew her mother was dead. She didn't cry, and I didn't make a sound. Instantly, I thought about my own mother. What if she died? Next morning, a group of men wearing skullcaps escorted the woman to her final resting place deep in the woods. What I witnessed that day intensified my fears of losing someone I loved, someone in my family.

Every morning, summer and winter, armed guards escorted the adults into the deep forest to cut trees. The fallen trees, cleared of all branches, were transported by horse and wagon to the banks of the Yenisey. They stayed there all winter until the spring thaw.

The guards insisted that we attend school. They were very strict about it. Sometimes, during unscheduled "visits," the guards found us hiding under the bunk beds and ordered us off to school.

It was a four-kilometer walk through the forest in an isolated settlement. We never walked to school alone, not even in pairs; it wasn't safe. Danger was always present, especially from animals. We trudged through the snows in groups of six or more. Sometimes, we heard wolves howling in the distance. We felt their presence. Often, we saw flickering lights shining through the shrubs. We knew those were the eyes of wolves watching us. Strangely, they never hurt us. They ran around in packs. We did too—a bunch of urchins with rags on our feet.

18
Sad Eyes

I liked school. It was a one-room, log-cabin schoolhouse for children of all ages. We made friends with native-born Russian children, and we learned the Russian alphabet.

Best of all, I liked the open hearth and the sweet scent of burning firewood that made the schoolroom smell wonderful. The warm hearth kept my hands and feet warm and my face tingling. Sometimes, it put me to sleep. The warmth of the fire reached the innermost core of your being. In a life with few comforts, this was probably the closest thing to heaven.

Every day, we got a chunk of bread for lunch. The sticky brown bread was a mysterious thing in itself. You never knew what you might find lodged inside it. It was not unusual to find pebbles, straw, or even sand mixed in with the bread.

There was no Santa Claus or Christmas in Siberia, but when Father Frost visited the school, it was probably the most exciting event of all for all of us children, little or not so little. He always handed out glazed honey cakes shaped like snowmen. What a treat that was!

The other log cabin in the settlement was the post office and health clinic. It had a good supply of zinc ointment—just about the only medicine that existed anywhere around—that was prescribed for ailments ranging from stomachache to earache, even the flu. "Just rub it in," we were always told.

I liked the bakery best of all. It was just a bread counter in the rear of the cabin. The women in white coats and caps grudgingly dispensed small portions of bread to those who had ration cards. We didn't have ration cards; we only went to school in the settlement. But Frydzia devised a system that seemed to work most of the time. After school, we would approach the bread counter and just stand there, quietly.

"Don't say a word," Frydzia instructed me. "Just look at the women with big, sad eyes, and don't leave till you get some bread."

I was unhappy begging for food. Frydzia always stood behind me, close enough for the women to know that we were together and that both of us were hungry. Her closeness gave me courage.

With grim faces that seemed to emphasize the self-importance of their posts behind the counter, the women stared back at us with disdain in their eyes. Still, I believed it was just an act because, most of the time, they were generous, giving us a chunk of bread and sending us on our way.

"Go, go," they would say and chase us out. Most of the time, we ate the bread right away, but sometimes, we brought it home to Mama and Papa. And most of the time, I didn't like what was happening in our lives.

Sometimes, I felt confused—the dissembling, the disdain, and the generosity, the very need to find our own bread ... I didn't understand any of it. Less than a year before—just a short while, as it seemed to me—we had been home with plenty to eat. Now, hunger was our daily companion.

Everything had changed. I had no inkling then how profoundly our lives had been upended. But I could sense— although I could not articulate—how completely I had been uprooted from the place and way of life I knew as home.

19
When Messiah Comes ...

From the moment we first arrived in Siberia and Papa took my hand—"Come, Sorele [my Hebrew name], we're going in," he said—I had balked at the idea, literally refusing to go inside. I didn't want to live with the rest of the relatives and with all the anger and argument that seemed to permeate our lives.

Cousin Simon was especially angry with my father, blaming him for everything that had happened to us. He blamed my father for "dragging us out of our homes" back in Nazi-occupied Poland and for "all our unhappiness and misfortunes," as Simon put it. Later, of course, it became clear that in "dragging" the family away, my father was responsible for saving all our lives, but in the miserable and desperate situation at the time, he received blame instead of gratitude.

And conditions were pretty miserable. Twelve of us—thirteen with the baby, Lily—lived in a one-room barracks.

Tante Bronia and Uncle Beno were in another barracks with strangers, only steps away from us. I didn't understand why I couldn't live with Tante Bronia. My father's youngest sister, Bronia, was my favorite aunt. Actually, she was funny looking—partly why I liked her so much. She had short legs and short arms, even a short nose that seemed perfectly centered in her round face.

There was always an aura of contentment about her. But best of all, Tante Bronia was always interested in what I had to say and what I liked to do. She gave me her undivided attention. It was she who had continued to tutor me in Polish when the war broke out and I could no longer go to school.

I liked Uncle Beno also. He was a very devout Talmud scholar. He managed to bring his treasured Talmud books with him all the way to Siberia. He studied the difficult passages whenever he wasn't cutting trees for the Soviets. Sometimes, he had a distant look in his eyes, as if he were contemplating the wisdom in his Talmud text. We could hear him chanting Hebrew prayers, even when he carried heavy buckets of water from the river or chopped wood for the stove that seemed to smoke more than it burned.

Sometimes, Uncle Beno gathered all of us young children and sat us down on the grass facing a wooded hill. "You see this mountain?" he would ask, pointing to the little hill. "When Messiah comes, he will part this mountain and take us all out of here like Moses. Did you know Moses parted the Red Sea and took the Hebrews out of Egypt? Well, he did. But in the meantime, while we are waiting for the Messiah, we must be good and do mitzvoth—good deeds." Uncle Beno always told the truth, so we believed without any doubt that Messiah would come very soon.

He was a very kind and gentle man, especially to the old people and young children. He never got involved in the family disputes; he wanted no part of them.

Bronia and Benjamin had no children of their own, but Bronia had seven nieces: from Bella, who was the same age as

Bronia, to Lily, the baby. Still, I believed my aunt Bronia liked me the best.

Although it was probably natural for me to want to live in Bronia and Beno's barracks, in some ways, I liked that they were next door. It gave me an opportunity to go visit. I would escape from our barracks to hear Tante Bronia recount wonderful stories about life back home before the war, especially about hiking in the Tatra Mountains. Or I would go there for lessons in reading and writing Polish or to hear Uncle Beno chanting phrases from the Hebrew text.

Our barracks had four large bunk beds with straw mats, one in each corner. As the authority figure of the family, my father claimed the best bunk in the room, the one near a window. All the others took the remaining three corners. There were complaints about this, discontent over the fact that some corners were near the door, which were not the best locations. I wasn't too fond of my relatives complaining so much, especially when it turned to anger that was directed at my father.

Our barracks was also home to millions of bugs. They were everywhere. They flew and crawled in through the door and the tiny window, but worst of all were the bugs that nestled in the grass stuffed between the logs of our barracks walls. They crawled out to torment us in the middle of the night. I felt invaded by the bugs.

Papa assumed the role of the elder person. He was not the oldest of the clan but the most decisive of them all. He instructed everyone to store all the belongings under the bunks, thereby clearing some of the space in the center of the room.

Baby Lily was only six months old. She cried often, keeping us awake at night. Maybe the awful bugs were horrible to her as well.

A cast-iron potbelly stove stood in the center of the barracks room. The stove was both a blessing and a curse. It kept us warm. A warm stove was a wonderful blessing, even in the summer. But it was a curse in that we couldn't cook much because the top of the stove was only big enough for one small pot. One pot for all thirteen of us! The women quarreled over the stove more than anything else. They arranged a "stove use" code. Mama was not good at it. Sometimes, I saw her crying. She was no match for those women in my father's family. They were fierce.

Mama was thirty-six at that time. She was very upset because she thought she might be pregnant. I knew this because I overheard Mama and Papa talking late one night and heard Mama saying this was the wrong time and place to have a baby. Then it turned out she was not pregnant after all. She got very skinny, probably because she often gave away her own ration of bread to the rest of us.

20
Papa the Old Man

Papa reached the age of thirty-nine and grew a long beard that turned gray. Although quite fit, he walked with a stick and told the Soviet guards he was old and ill. They called him "*dyedushka*,"—"granddaddy" in Russian. This gave him a definite advantage. When the guards were not looking, he would escape from the line of workers marching into the woods. There, instead of cutting trees for the Soviets, he searched for food.

Papa grew a beard, Siberian camp

Sometimes, Papa did not return until the following morning. He said he knew some people in the nearest settlement who gave him food for the family. I never learned who those people were.

I understood that my father seemed always to come up with ideas; he was resourceful and knew how to solve even the most difficult problems.

Mama seemed passive most of the time, believing in fate—what needed to happen would happen—so different from Papa. He was not complaisant and did not quite believe in fate. He believed that he could improve our lives, even take certain risks to make things better.

Mama was only content when she could feed her family, especially her two little girls. That is when all was well with the world and she was at peace with herself and everyone around her.

Whenever Papa did not return to the barracks before nightfall, Mama always made excuses.

"Don't worry," she would say, "Papa is safe. He'll be home first thing in the morning. It's not safe to travel through the woods in the middle of the night." Her explanation sounded ambiguous. I didn't understand why she wasn't even a little upset.

But Papa always did return home to us, sometimes carrying bread. Sometimes, he brought fresh fish. He would say he caught the fish with his bare hands. Then he would laugh that charming, exuberant laughter. His capacity for laughter was unique, especially under difficult circumstances. I remember Jewish people being more modest in expressing something amusing. Not my father! His laughter always made me think of a Tartar or a Kazakh laughing like that.

Even in summer, food was hard to find. Again, one summer morning, Papa left the barracks early and was not back by evening. This time, Mama seemed really upset. Did she know something? Was she worried that maybe this time he wasn't coming back at all?

We stayed up all night waiting for him, not knowing what might have happened. Mama did not communicate her concerns to my sister and me. Frydzia and I worried that he was stranded in the forest, hurt and alone. We understood that to be lost in those woods at night was like being lost at sea. But Mama was still firm in her belief that Papa was not stranded in the woods.

Next morning, there was a loud knock on the door. There, for everyone to see, stood my father, alive and smiling, holding a fish in his hand. His smile was mainly directed at my mother. He ignored all the others. No one said anything; they just all stared at him. Papa kept smiling at Mama—his shy, apologetic smile that said, *Forgive me for being out all night.*

The fish in his hand was a whole smoked salmon, maybe one foot long. He told us how he had stumbled upon a small settlement outpost at the edge of the river and discovered a group of men busily smoking fish over a fire in an open pit. They gave him the fish, he said, although he most probably traded something of ours for it.

Clothing for food was a common transaction; my mother had already given up all her silk underwear and nightgowns for food, and the Russian women back in Lwow and Brzuchowice had worn my mother's nightgowns as dresses.

Papa kept looking at Mama and pointing to the fish as if to say, *We will have a feast today!*

Well, I think it was the smug look on my father's face that sent Cousin Simon over the edge. His anger knew no limit; he became apoplectic with rage.

"You mean you're going to eat the whole fish all by yourselves?" he screamed. "It's you who took us out of our homes. It's you who is responsible for all of us being banished here in this godforsaken land!"

Papa just stood there. He said nothing. The fish was still in his hand as he turned around and walked out the door, taking the fish with him. Mama ran after him. Frydzia started crying. I was very upset but tried hard not to cry.

21
A Field of Potatoes

Papa returned to the barracks that same evening but without the fish. He told everyone to sit down because he had something important to tell us all. He said he had gone back to the remote spot at the edge of the river and had again found the men at the smoking pit. He explained that one fish could not feed all fifteen people, so would they please make another trade, this time for some other food. The men agreed it was a reasonable request. After debating among themselves, the men came up with a solution.

"*Khorosho*," said the men, the Russian word for "very good" or "okay."

"We will give you a whole field of potatoes for the fish," they said. Papa was overjoyed but at the same time disbelieving this sudden good fortune. How could that be, a whole field of potatoes for a small fish? A field of potatoes could feed an army!

Finally, the men dropped the bomb—the other part of the deal.

"You see," they said, "it's late in the summer, and all the potatoes are long dug out and hauled away, but if you are willing to dig deep enough and hard enough, you will dig up enough potatoes to feed your family for many days—maybe even weeks." Papa agreed to the trade.

The family was overjoyed. Everyone thought it was such a brilliant trade!

Next evening, armed with old burlap sacks and old rags, we went out to dig in the potato field. We dug late into the night. We were lucky because the days were long during the summer in Siberia. It didn't get even vaguely dark until very late at night. The sun seemed only half-hidden beyond the horizon, never really disappearing completely. Its glow made the night seem like day. Next evening, we went out again to dig in the field. Just as we had the night before, we came back with lots of potatoes.

We ate potatoes for breakfast, lunch, and supper. Sometimes, we ate them boiled, but mostly, we ate them baked over an open fire in the clearing. For days, we ate practically nothing but potatoes. Our hunger was gone, but all of us grew bloated and then sick with diarrhea. We were sick for days. What to do?

In Siberia, there were no medicines for any ailments— except for zinc ointment. Well, zinc ointment did not cure our potato sickness. It took several days, but we all got better, even Lily. Best of all, no one was angry at my father anymore, until next time when he was again blamed for "dragging" us from our homes and for being banished in the "godforsaken" land of Siberia.

22
To Central Asia, 1941

Hitler invaded the USSR in June 1941. As a child, I only learned about the invasion from a song we sang that went like this—"22 June, exactly 4:00 a.m., they bombed Kiev and declared war." But I didn't know about millions of Hitler's Axis troops that stormed into the Soviet Union along an 1,800-mile front extending from Finland down the Baltic states, north to Leningrad, Minsk, Smolensk, and Ukraine and the Caucasus in the south. The Red Army was unprepared for the onslaught of the highly trained, highly experienced Axis forces, and the population was unprepared for the mass carnage systematically carried out—especially against Jews by the Nazi Einsatzgruppen, the SS killing squads—in the wake of initial German military successes. Civilian murders and starvation were staggering, and the human suffering seemed endless.

Shortly after the invasion of Soviet Union by Nazi Germany, Stalin declared amnesty for most foreign nationals imprisoned in Siberian work camps. That meant we could leave as soon as we obtained the proper documents. But where could we go? Not back home. Home was where the Nazis were. All through the eastern part of Poland, in Belarus and Ukraine, the German Army was winning on all fronts.

We also needed to get away from the cold. Another Siberian winter would be devastating. That summer of 1941, food was all the family talked about—how to get some for the coming winter, how to store some for the journey. In the meantime, we ate whatever we found growing in the clearing around the camp and in the woods. Mama arranged mushrooms on strings and dried them outside in the sun, hanging them on nails fastened to the side of our barracks. She stashed away grain and dry fish in a small burlap bag—preparation for moving on.

We needed to arrange for transportation. Papa seemed to know the map of the Soviet Union by heart. The amnesty order said we were allowed to travel eastward, but Siberia was so huge that you could travel eastward for a long time and still be in Siberia; instead, Papa focused on central Asia. It too was part of the Soviet Union, and because it was warm most of the year, he thought it would be a good choice. It was always easier to find food—and to survive a war—in milder climates.

By August of that summer, members of the whole clan had packed up their belongings, and we set out on our way. I recall riding in a horse-drawn wagon again. We hoped to reach a railway station, but it was a long way to Krasnoyarsk, and we knew that, once there, we might have to wait days before boarding a train.

There were very few trains in Siberia, which had one lifeline: the Trans-Siberian Railroad, spanning the entire European Soviet Union all the way east to the Pacific Ocean. With the beginning of the German-Soviet conflict in 1941, a train schedule ceased to exist. Sometimes passengers waited many days at the rail stations along the entire system.

What's more, that summer, Russian civilians were in flight from the Germans and the battlefields; they had become refugees like us, so Russians by the tens of thousands were also fleeing east.

⁓

Far from the fighting, our wagon traveled a narrow dirt road through the peaceful forest; the sound of the wheels turning slowly was especially comforting. Our first day on the road was a long one. It was that time of the year when summer days never seemed to end and nights never came. We were tired and needed a place to rest. Suddenly, a log cabin appeared in the distance, and then another. Maybe they would let us in. Mama told us to follow her out of the wagon. She knocked on the door. I felt small before the massive door.

"Look straight into the eyes of the person who opens the door," Mama told us. "The people in this region are kind to children. So, for the sake of the children, they will let us in." I knew Mama was right. I always thought I would be rewarded with kindness when looking into people's eyes. Perhaps I thought that most adults in Siberia felt a natural affinity with children, especially children in need.

Slowly, the heavy door creaked open. An old woman stood in the doorway, staring at us. I stared back at her. Her long, braided brown hair mixed with silver seemed to have escaped from under her scarf-covered head. The long, coarse cloth skirt she wore and bare feet seemed odd to me.

In her broken Russian, Mama pleaded with the woman to let us in. The woman hesitated at first, cast a quick glance back into the hut, and then opened the door wide and motioned us in. Papa followed quietly.

It was only a one-room hut, but it was big, with several small windows built into the log walls. Tiny rays of light shining through the windows provided a feeling of warmth. The room was sparsely furnished—a couple of cots, a small wooden table covered with a white, crocheted tablecloth, only two or three chairs. A large oven, maybe as tall as I was, was built into the corner of the room. A blanket was draped over the top of the oven. I had seen this type of oven before, although I could not remember where. It looked like it was built of dry clay mixed with straw. I knew it served as a bed for the night when it was no longer lit.

We stared at the oven, so warm and inviting. The old woman pointed to a bench near the oven and told us to sit and rest. She pulled up a low wooden stool, sat down, and spread her arms wide. A young boy—he could have been my age—with fair skin and hair and gentle features walked over and settled down in her lap. She wrapped her arms around him and whispered in his ear. It was a pretty picture. They looked so content. I envied their closeness. Maybe she was telling him a fairy tale, and I strained to listen.

But then, something happened. Their contentment disappeared, and both the woman and the boy suddenly seemed distraught. Immediately, I knew this was no fairy tale. I overheard her telling the boy that she, his grandmother, would most probably die very soon. "*Babushka budiet skoro umierat*," she said. The boy stared at her, motionless in her embrace. I felt so sad. I turned to my mother.

"Mama, why does Babushka have to die?"

"Because she is old," Mama answered.

"How old?" I asked.

"Fifty, maybe fifty-five."

"But Mama, I don't want Babushka to die. What will happen to the little boy? He will be alone."

Mama moved closer to me. Gently, she touched my arm.

"That's life, my child," she answered.

23
No Train Tickets

We moved on to Krasnoyarsk and waited many days at the rail station for a train to take us south to central Asia. There were no train tickets available because the system was in total chaos. There would be standing room only—if we were lucky. The trains heading east and south were especially packed, we were told.

Like everyone else, we would simply try to hitch a ride, just push our way inside a train. The passenger trains had been pressed into service as troop transports, taking Soviet soldiers west to the front, known as the eastern front during World War II. We understood that we would most probably ride in a cattle train again.

At last, a train—a passenger train, actually—pulled into the Krasnoyarsk station, snaking its way along the entire length of the platform. It was no small task to push our way in. It was packed to capacity with human cargo, and a thick odor of sweat seemed to spread like a steamy cloud above our heads. Who could bathe in those days? That was an unattainable luxury.

Mama and Papa gripped our wrists and held on to our meager belongings as if with vengeance. Their facial expressions were hard and determined, and their hands felt like steel bands around my wrist. Losing a loved one, being separated even for a moment in those awful, dark days of war was tragic. To this day, I remember the haunting cries of children crying out, "Mama, Mama, Papa!"—hysterical crying that pierced your heart.

We pushed our way into a railroad car that had standing room only. No one was there to check for travel permits or train tickets. No one cared. Some people traveled on the rooftops of the railroad cars. They appeared like a tight mass of humanity holding on to each other. Some were still standing on the metal stairs that led up to the cars, gripping the railing, as the train pulled out of the station.

We were all in flight. People from every corner of Belarus, Ukraine, and western Russia were fleeing east and then south, away from the Nazi atrocities back home. In addition to their fear and anguish, many carried another feeling: surprise.

Before the Nazi invasion of the Soviet Union, many of these people—and especially the Ukrainians—had longed to be "liberated" from the Soviet political system, such was their hatred of the Bolsheviks. In addition, Ukrainians were traditionally not fond of the Jews, so they were sympathetic to Hitler's goal of getting rid of Jews. They had no idea, however, that Nazis considered the Slavs subhumans, only a notch above the Jews. The Ukrainians continued to look forward to their arrival.

I recall an incident in the fall of 1939, when we were fleeing from Poland and were in Ukrainian territory. My mother spotted an orchard full of ripe walnuts.

"Can you spare a few walnuts for my children?" Mama pleaded.

"No," the woman in the orchard responded. "These walnuts are for the Germans when they finally arrive."

Well, they got there. And nothing had prepared the local population for the brutality the Germans visited on the waiting Ukrainians. People were tortured and hung. Towns and villages were plundered and burned, creating hundreds of thousands of civilian refugees. Those who escaped with their lives headed eastward, packing trains like ours beyond capacity.

Our extended family followed a strict rule: under difficult circumstances, all the adults were responsible only for their immediate family, and all would hope to be reunited at some point of disembarkation, so we could not know for certain whether or not all our relatives managed to board the same train we had taken from Krasnoyarsk.

Train travel in those days took forever—not hours but days or weeks. Frequently, the locomotive was disengaged from the rest of the train, and we were held on the sidetracks, thus freeing up the main tracks for trains heading in the opposite direction, transporting troops to fight the Germans in the west.

Weeks went by. Summer turned to autumn. Inside our compartment was no longer so steamy hot, no longer so packed with refugees. Many had disembarked along the way, and for the first time, we had our own seats, sometimes by the window but not always together. We slept sitting up, sometimes squeezing our feet onto each other's seats or into each other's laps. We had little food and water. Sometimes, Mama brought hot water from the train engineer in the steam locomotive. We drank the hot water, which wasn't clean, pretending that it was teatime.

I have no idea how Mama and Papa kept up their spirits and their strength yet managed to keep us all safe and together. They spoke little. To speak was too exhausting. Their eyes were always watchful. We clung to each other. It seemed logical to me that if we let go, we would lose one another, and we would lose ourselves.

At the age of eight, I believed that I could protect my family by making sure that we remained in our tiny space in the railroad car. How could I know at that young age that my need to protect them was in fact my need to be protected myself?

⁓

Our first stop was Novosibirsk, the largest Siberian city. We got off the train. I have few recollections of that particular station. I do remember that we took refuge on the floor, finding a small space to sit inside the enormous station. I also remember a young woman in a white uniform who approached our little "camp." She addressed herself specifically to my mother.

Before long, maybe half an hour later, Frydzia and I were marched off with the woman—away from our parents.

I could not cry, but inside, I was hysterical. My heart was pounding. My stomach and some of its contents were in my mouth. I needed to go to the bathroom. Instead, I wet myself. Everything that could happen to me physically and emotionally was happening right at that moment.

The woman seemed warm, sincere. "You will see your parents tomorrow," she said, trying to reassure us. Of course, I did not believe her. She led us up a huge stone staircase into an enormous room filled with empty beds—not a person in sight. To add to our tremendous distress at not knowing what was happening, we were now entering a dormitory room that seemed to me eerie and frightening.

As always, Frydzia, my big, brave sister, tried to reassure me, whispering and nodding her head, her big brown eyes expressing almost maternal feelings. Her eyes were saying, *We are in this together; I will take care of you.*

The lady led us toward a couple of beds. I was surprised at how beautiful those beds were—more beautiful than I had seen in a long time. They were metal, crib-style beds painted white, with railings on each side. They appeared to be beds for young children. She pointed out two beds side by side.

"These beds will be yours for tonight," she said, and she smiled. Then something happened that made me feel reassured.

I glanced toward the headboard, and what I saw amazed me. There, in full view, was a red ribbon arranged in the shape of a large red rose. It was so beautiful. Suddenly, I felt that I could trust the woman in the white uniform. I believed that she was offering us a restful night—something so unusual in those days of war.

I had not slept in a bed of my own with clean sheets and blankets in more than two years. I believed that she would indeed return us to our parents—tomorrow. And, of course, that is exactly what happened. The following morning, we were reunited with Mama and Papa.

It was late September or early October when we arrived in Alma-Ata, present-day Almaty, Kazakhstan. At last, we arrived in central Asia, the "warmer" place my father believed would be the best location to wait out the war.

But first, we waited in the station. The train remained in the station for many hours. At least by now, my parents knew exactly which cars the other family members were traveling in. A terrible windstorm was blowing sand everywhere—a wind so ferocious that it darkened the sky above us. The family convened and made a quick decision to travel farther south to Uzbekistan, perhaps even farther to Tajikistan.

And that is what we did. We traveled on and then all disembarked in Tashkent, Uzbekistan. We settled down on the grass in a park in the center of town, where every bit of space was taken up by refugees from everywhere, especially from the western parts of the Soviet Union. Unknown to us, however, both the grass and the people around us were crawling with lice—a constant reality of the war and the perfect vehicle for spreading disease.

So like thousands of others, we went to sleep—all fifteen of us—on the grass that first night in the park. And like thousands of others, we woke up the next morning seriously infested with lice. In addition to that, Uncle Beno was particularly upset to discover that his pocket watch had been stolen right off him while he was sleeping.

There was one other thing about this theft that was both sad and funny: Uncle Beno was covered from head to toe in a white powder. Some people thought the white powder was used to induce a sound sleep, and we assumed the thieves had used it to ensure their getaway with Uncle Beno's watch. Unfortunately, thievery was the norm in those times. Survival of the fittest was the rule.

24
Tajikistan

One good thing happened to us in the park. We bumped into Yohanan, a cousin from back home. He and some members of his family had found their way to Leninabad (present-day Khujand), Tajikistan. A small community of refugees like us had already made their home in Leninabad, and Yohanan encouraged us to join them. We all packed into a truck and headed for Leninabad.

Khujand (Leninabad) is very close to the Afghanistan border and sits on the Syr Darya River at the mouth of the Fergana Valley. Its climate is mild, although it is hot in summer, but it does not experience the fierce winds of the steppes of Kazakhstan.

The Tajik people were the largest ethnic group inhabiting that part of the Soviet Union. They were unlike any people we had seen or known before, and they were very wary of us.

The people of Siberia had never exhibited any prejudice against others. They fought the elements in nature and tried to survive; they had no time for intolerance.

The Tajik people, on the other hand, were suspicious of strangers—people of different religions, people who looked different from themselves. Sunni Muslims, they viewed us with suspicion as "infidels." Dark skinned and dark eyed, they were also suspicious of people with light skin, blue eyes, and blond hair, who were rarely seen in that part of the world.

Immediately, I was struck by the absence of women. This was a man's world! Later, I learned that women preferred to stay in the background—in their homes, if possible. Men and boys in their quilted and often brightly embroidered caftans and head coverings, called *tibitayka,* dominated the narrow dirt streets and stucco-walled alleyways.

Occasionally, one could glimpse a couple of women, never alone, covered head to toe in black *pranga,* the caftan. These women could only see as much of the outside world as the long black netting attached to the front of their caftans allowed. Young or old, ugly or beautiful, a Tajik woman was seen only by her very close friends and relatives and only in her own surroundings. Little girls dressed like adult women but without the face cover. Sometimes, one could see them squatting low against a wall in the narrow streets, chatting with friends or taking a rest.

Their customs seemed strange to us—and vice versa. For the most part, the Tajik people did not like us. As soon as they learned that we were Jewish, they began calling us "Zhid." Yet they were tolerant of the Bukharian Jews, a small minority who had lived among them for many centuries.

The Bukharian men and women, their skin darker than ours, were very handsome people. Unlike the Tajiks, the Bukharian men did not wear the caftan. Rather, they dressed in the baggy slacks and shirts typical of the region—not the trim slacks and shirts of Western style.

However, the Bukharian men always wore head coverings— large skullcaps, colorfully embroidered, or just black skullcaps embroidered in white. Their women did not cover their faces, but modesty was important; they wore vibrant-hued long and loose dresses of handwoven silk. Under the dresses, they wore harem-style slacks, and silk scarves covered their long, braided hair.

Some women wore beautiful gold jewelry—gold chains around their necks, earrings, bracelets on their wrists, and rings on their fingers. Having so much gold spelled prosperity—being of the upper class.

Leninabad was also home to the smallest minority, the true Russians who had emigrated there in recent years. Unlike the Tajiks, who were mostly tradespeople, the Russians were better educated; many were professionals.

When we first arrived, we were dependent on the small Jewish community from back home for food and a place to lay our heads down.

But like us, they had very little to spare. Soon, our very survival depended on the generosity of Bukharian Jews. Often, they shared their food with us. I still remember the pungent aroma of rice pilaf cooked with bits of lamb, carrots, and spices of the Orient. I can still taste it—in my memory. Their bread, for instance—the round, flat *lepioshka* with tiny black seeds in the center—remains the best bread of all. For me, it is maybe even a symbol of survival.

25
Kibitka, Our Hut

Late in 1941, before the winter rains turned the hot, dusty streets into mud, Papa found us a place of our own—a hut, or *kibitka,* with a dirt floor and walls of hardened dirt mixed with straw.

The one room had a low ceiling, two cots, a small table, one small, iron stove, and a little kerosene lamp. During scorching summer days, we washed the dirt floor with a bucket of water. The water seeped into the dirt floor and kept our little room cool all day long. Our hut was part of a compound with a courtyard. The owners of the property allowed us to use the courtyard, which was a blessing on hot summer days and nights.

The narrow dirt alleyways of Leninabad were lined with hardened dirt walls, heavy doorways here and there, with no windows anywhere to be seen. Who knew there were homes behind those walls? Those streets were extremely claustrophobic, twisting every which way with no particular logic, sometimes just leading to vacant and foreboding stretches of land. It seemed so strange, so uninviting.

We lived in the old part of town on a crooked, narrow alleyway, Madanyat 195, which ran perpendicular to a wider street called Lahuti, always crowded with shoppers and Tajik men riding their donkeys, seated on "saddles" that were doubled-up carpet bags. Sometimes, the donkeys were encouraged to gallop, usually with a gentle and sometimes not-so-gentle kick to the belly of the poor animal.

Mama warned Frydzia and me to be careful at all times. "Never enter deserted places," she always told us. I was still very young, but she was determined to keep her little girls safe from abuse by strangers. She was especially uneasy about sexual abuse. The women in the region were in some ways protected from sexual abuse by the clothes they wore. We did not wear such clothes.

But as we grew taller, our dresses got shorter, and with our bare legs, we were more at risk for sexual abuse. One day, she brought home some fabric from some place, I've no idea where. By hand, she sewed a piece of fabric into the hemline of our dresses. Mama was pleased to see us in dresses that reached below our knees.

She worried so much about our safety in the streets. I think she wished that she could keep us locked up in the hut. Maybe she was right. In some ways, we were like baby animals in the wild. You either survived or you didn't. It was a wilderness out there; that was something I did not understand as a child.

So Mama taught us well in the best school of all—the school of survival. "Lusia, don't look at me like that," she would say to me. "You think you are cute with those innocent blue eyes, but that alone will not keep you safe. If you see two or more boys or young men, turn around and walk—or better yet, run—the other way. They will not hurt you if they don't see you, so stay out of sight."

I learned well and knew never to enter deserted places. But I learned soon enough that crowded streets were not always a safe haven for little girls.

Sometimes, inappropriate touching occurred in full view of others—people who did not intervene or respond in any way to a child's cry for help. Such was the culture of that land. Still, I felt much more secure in crowded streets, as opposed to deserted places. Vacant or abandoned spaces—there were many of them in old Leninabad—frightened me the most.

One day, I took a shortcut crossing a vacant lot on my way to school. I saw a man and a woman in a tight embrace leaning against a wall. I was not quite nine years old and very naive about sexuality. Only later did I understand that the two people in their passionate embrace were having sex. But at the time, I believed they were doing something I wasn't supposed to witness. I needed to run fast, and I did. I ran faster than ever in my entire life.

One day, as it was bound to happen, I had to fight off a stranger who was touching me inappropriately. The Tajik man was young, maybe even a teenager. He grabbed me from behind and managed to hold me with just one hand. His grip was like steel around my middle. With his other hand he tried to reach under my dress. I screamed, which attracted a lot of attention.

I managed to free myself by kicking and scratching. He didn't like being scratched, so he let go and slapped my face. Then he laughed. For him, it was a game. But for me, the awareness, the very experience of being assaulted that way, became all too real.

Mama was right; it was a wilderness out there in those streets. Over time, I learned to protect myself. I was mindful of men watching me or following me too closely. I was a fast runner and learned to look for ways of escape, usually by darting down crowded alleyways. Finally, I understood my mother's warnings.

26
Rachel and Her Family

Our immediate neighbors, a family of Bukharian Jews, owned our hut and the rest of the compound. The matriarch of the family next door, Rachel, was probably in her forties. She was older than my mother. Her husband had run away in the 1920s, in the early years of Bolshevik ascendance. He fled to Palestine through Persia and promised to send for his family. Sadly, it did not work out that way.

Rachel's oldest son, Abram, maybe in his twenties, was the man in his family in every sense of the word. Abram was very resourceful. He was an entrepreneur, which, in the Soviet Union, was frowned upon; indeed, it was illegal most of the time. But Abram provided a decent livelihood for his mother and his two younger sisters, Sara and Zina, by dealing in foreign currency, an activity strictly forbidden under Soviet law. So, while providing for his family, Abram was also risking his own life and theirs due to his profession.

It was through Abram's profession that I glimpsed, for the first time and only for a brief moment, the US currency. In my mind, everything American was strong and solid, and the American money looked solid to me.

I liked Abram a lot. He was strong and handsome. His strength meant stability to me. I thought, how wonderful that my father's name was Abraham, a name which was very common among Ashkenazi Jews, and that Abram was the same name among Bukharian Jews. It felt good, as if there were a real kinship between us.

We were strangers in that land, and we were strangers to them. Only several weeks earlier, they hadn't even known us, yet they took us in, and more than that, they took us into their hearts. It really felt like we were family.

For us, an invitation to supper was a lifesaver. I recall how we sat in a circle, their family and ours, on the floor covered with Oriental rugs. We ate, all of us using our fingers only, from one common platter full of aroma-filled, steaming rice pilaf.

They were good people. Sometimes, it seemed to me that they assumed responsibility for us. They did not believe that we were savvy enough to understand that land and its people, which indeed was true. Both the land and the people were foreign to us in so many ways. Papa did not have a clue how to earn money and not get caught by the police. Most activities that people engaged in were illegal. Anything legal did not put food on the table. We were running out of things to trade for food.

27
Winter 1941/42

We settled into our tiny hut under difficult conditions. Mama and Papa shared one cot, and Frydzia and I shared the other. The cots were so narrow that it was impossible to turn from side to side without the other person turning as well. I slept rolled into a fetal position, with Frydzia spooned around me, her body pressed into mine, her arm resting on my thigh or the nook of my waist. This is how we always slept. I couldn't fall asleep any other way. Frydzia and I needed privacy, with Papa sleeping only a few feet away, so we all perfected a technique of dressing and undressing under our bedding.

Life was a struggle that first winter. We had little food, no running water—actually, no one had running water or electricity in the old town of Leninabad. The only source of light during long winter nights was a kerosene lamp, which we used sparingly. Like everything else, kerosene was available in the black market at exorbitant prices. It was such a joy sitting around the table when the lamp was lit. Our small, iron stove stayed cold most of the time for lack of firewood. The cheapest and more available kindling—flat, round cakes of dry manure mixed with straw—burned well in the stove but gave off a terrible smell. Most of the time, we preferred wearing our coats to lighting the smelly stove. Fortunately, the winters were short, usually ending in late February.

But we were besieged by infectious diseases. People everywhere that savage winter of the war were dying of typhus, tuberculosis, malaria, and dysentery. Typhus—caused by lice, which were everywhere—was the most dreaded disease of all and the number-one killer that winter. Members of our extended family were not immune.

Cousin Solomon—the father of Syma, Frydzia, and Lily—came down with typhus and was dead the next day, and he was only in his early thirties. The family escorted him to the Bukharian burial grounds. The women and children stood behind a stone fence, along with Uncle Beno—who was Solomon's brother. As a Cohen (the priestly and most noble caste), Uncle Beno was not allowed near the grave, as Cohens were not allowed contact with the dead. So he stood with us women behind the stone fence, climbing to the top of a large stone, struggling as he leaned over to catch a glimpse of his brother's burial.

This was the first time I had gone to a funeral. I could not understand why someone young and healthy like Cousin Solomon, who only a day earlier had carried two buckets of water, was not returning home with us. I had seen death before. I saw dead people after the bombings when we were fleeing into eastern Poland, and I saw dead people in Siberia. I understood that the sleep of the dead didn't look like ordinary sleep.

Cousin Bella, Solomon's young widow, couldn't provide for her three little girls, so she placed the two older ones, Syma and Frydzia, in an orphanage. While her mother worked in a factory, little Lily was cared for by her grandparents, Tante Esther and Uncle Benjamin.

Uncle Beno came down with typhus next. With great effort, Papa managed to buy the right medicine in the black market. Uncle Beno survived.

Doctors were powerless to help the sick and dying. There were no medicines available, except in the black market. The Russian doctors made house calls, but they were as poor as everyone else and often accepted food as payment. One time when Papa was sick with very high fever, Mama offered the visiting doctor some watery soup. He graciously accepted and sat down, and without any words spoken between them, he ate the soup and departed.

Papa was the first in our immediate family to come down with typhus; at least, the doctor believed that's what it was but conceded that he could not be 100 percent sure.

During his delirium, Papa kept pointing to one particular spot on the wall. He tried desperately to tell us something— something about the wall and something about keeping us safe. Papa eventually recovered, even without medicines. Days later, he explained his incoherent babblings. Apparently, he had carved a hole in the dirt wall of our hut where he had stashed two gold coins "for a rainy day." Two gold coins was a treasure. I didn't know we owned such wealth. He explained that these gold coins must never be traded for bread. They were to be used only if our lives were in danger. Possibly, we were to use the gold coins to bribe our way out of the Soviet Union.

There was more to this—a whole itinerary of possibilities. Papa thought we might be able to cross the border into Afghanistan and, from there, take a route to Iran. In Iran, he explained, we could conceivably hook up with the Anders Army, led by General Wladyslaw Anders, whose troops were reforming themselves as the exiled Polish army with a sizable contingent of Polish civilians. They were crossing via the Persian corridor into Iran, Iraq, and Palestine to join up with the British to fight the Nazis in North Africa. Papa believed that being Polish as well and speaking the Polish language, we might possibly be a part of that transport and just might reach Palestine somehow.

I believed with all my heart that this most exciting adventure would take place and that the dream of reaching Palestine would come true. Unfortunately, Wladyslaw Anders and his troops were known for being openly anti-Semitic, as was quite common in the Polish army and among the Polish soldiers. Papa wisely gave up on that whole idea of reaching Palestine.

My mother carried the dream in the shape of a seashell. It had been sent to her in Poland in the early 1930s by her best friend who had moved to Palestine. Mama held on to it throughout the long and difficult years of the war. I have it still, and to this day, we all treasure the shell. If you tap it gently against a hard surface, you will hear the sound of ocean waves.

28
Spring 1942

Tante Bronia got a job in a factory processing fruit into preserves. The fruit, called *uriuk*, was similar in taste to apricots but smaller and much sweeter. It was the best fruit locally grown and was most frequently processed into preserves. Tante Bronia's job was a godsend. Any job in the food-processing or food-packaging industry was a godsend. It was not the wages; they barely enabled workers to feed their families. No, it was the food that was stolen from the workplace that made a difference. It would either be eaten or traded for other necessities.

We were fortunate; Tante Bronia brought us delicious preserves from time to time. A little bit of preserve on a small piece of bread was pure heaven. But we worried about her. It was dangerous to steal on the job. Men and women in white coats were posted in the workplace for the sole purpose of watching for pilferage. You had to be clever and hide the stolen goods very carefully.

It was about this time, in the spring of 1942, that we were awakened very early one morning to a tremor that made our cots shake and move about, a tremor that felt like a real earthquake. Light tremors and earthquakes are not uncommon in that part of the world; sometimes they occur several times a year. What was terribly alarming that particular morning was that we were all awakened from a sound sleep, but Mama was nowhere to be seen! Our hut was shaking, our cots with us in them were moving about, and Mama was gone!

Papa was beside himself. He swayed and staggered about the hut, trying to reach the door. He ran out into the courtyard, all the time calling her name, "Raisil, Raisil, where are you?" It was horrible to see him so distraught. He was crying, although he tried hard not to show it.

Mama returned hours later carrying a large chunk of bread. He screamed at her, "Where were you? Where were you?" She tried hard to explain that she got up at four o'clock that morning to stand in a breadline, but before she could finish a sentence, Papa grabbed a chair and, in a temporary fit of madness, smashed it against a wall. He screamed so loudly! He was incoherent while Mama just stood there patiently waiting for him to calm down.

Frydzia and I sat up in our cot. We held each other in a tight embrace, not knowing what else we could do. I was so frightened. I had never seen my father display such rage. Was this rage more than anything directed at himself? Was it his inability to provide for his family the most basic needs of daily living? Or was it that my father understood better than anyone the dangers that existed for women in the narrow streets and alleyways of that land, especially for women unaccompanied by men?

That same year of 1942, my sister and I started school for the first time in Leninabad. I was almost nine years old, and Mama, as usual, worried about education, rather the lack of it, for her girls. But first, she found a friend for me. Her name was Bronia—like my favorite aunt—and she too was going on nine. It was great having a friend of my own. I hadn't had friends in years, since the war broke out. After all, when you are always on the run, you are lucky to get to keep your own family.

Leninabad class photo, Lusia front-row center (white blouse), Frydzia back-row on the right of the English-language instructor.

We learned from the family of my new friend that the expatriates from Poland were establishing a school. It was a Polish school; everything was taught in the Polish language, but it was based on the Soviet system and the Soviet curriculum.

In addition to being taught the Polish language, great Polish poets like Mickiewicz, and Polish novelists like Sienkewicz, we also recited poetry by Pushkin, the renowned Russian poet. Later, English-language instruction was introduced, as well as social sciences and mathematics. Later still, we learned algebra, geometry, chemistry, and physics. Yet Soviet propaganda was a very important "subject" in our school, as much as in all other Soviet schools.

Our school was small in size and numbers. We were perhaps one hundred students to about twelve teachers. The students in each class ranged in different ages; some students were two or three years older than others. I was one of the youngest and smallest kids in class.

Our teachers were not educators by profession; rather, they were educated men and women who had held various professions before the war—engineers, university professors, writers, chemists, and journalists, all from Poland. We did have two Russian teachers. Serafina Vasilyevna, who was actually a Tartar, taught us the Russian language and literature. I remember her with great pleasure. She was always cheerful, always smiling. When she smiled, her narrow, slanted eyes seemed closed and unseeing. I liked Serafina Vasilyevna. I believe I liked all smiling people.

Tovarish Ivanov—*tovarish,* of course, means *comrade*—a strong and muscular man who often wore a tank top, I think to show off his powerful muscles, was our gym teacher. He also taught us war studies. He used to make a great show of taking apart a rifle and displaying all the parts. "*Szkenty i knopki, szkenty i knopki.*" He would call out the various rifle parts, and we would repeat them by rote. For the subject of war studies, Tovarish Ivanov was properly attired in a Soviet uniform and a peaked cap with a red star on top.

In some ways, our school was like a private school, and we were fortunate in that we were given a very good education. And there was no such thing as elective subjects; everything was compulsory. But the best of all was the piece of bread and a bowl of soup we received daily.

Some of our teachers, notwithstanding their high educational achievements, were lacking in the empathy we needed in those most difficult circumstances. Some of them believed that suffering quietly was noble. Discussing feelings and physical or emotional problems was frowned upon. Some of them believed that pride built character and that one had to face suffering with dignity.

Many of us shared two dreadful afflictions—we were hungry, and we were infested with lice. Yet people rarely referred to either of these conditions with any degree of sympathy. The issue of lice infestation was raised in private, however. We were threatened in no uncertain terms with having our hair shaved off unless the plague of lice was resolved. I was in constant fear of having my thick hair cut off.

Mother poured naphtha all over our heads. It left our hair greasy and awful smelling, even after washing with soap containing lye. This awful treatment worked for a few days, maybe even a week or two; then we got infested all over again from other kids in school.

Being hungry was perhaps the worst affliction of all. Some teachers showed very little empathy for those kids who came to school without breakfast and unprepared for rigorous studies.

Leninabad class photo, Lusia front-row, first on the left, Frydzia middle-row third on the right

I vividly recall the time a friend was humiliated before the entire class by a teacher who rebuked her for not getting her homework done. "Maybe because you were hungry is why you came to school unprepared?" he asked, his voice dripping with sarcasm. The implication was that discomfort was no excuse for not doing one's work. But, truth be told, hunger was more than a discomfort.

Our immune systems were seriously compromised. We suffered from vitamin deficiency. We developed pustules and sores on our bodies, painful cracks in our lips and corners of our mouths, and watery eyes. We suffered all types of infection, from bacterial to fungal and even parasitic. And hunger did interfere with normal brain function. Besides, how do you work on mathematics or language when you're thinking about bread all day long?

When slices of bread were being portioned out and some students got bigger slices than others, we all knew not to say anything, to act as if it didn't matter. In fact, it did matter. It was an important piece of bread.

There were funny moments in school as well. Our English teacher, a young man educated at Oxford University in the United Kingdom, introduced us to a concept entirely new to anyone whose native tongue was Polish or Russian—the definite or indefinite article preceding a noun. The whole idea of "a" or "an" and "the" was unclear to us. Also, any word starting with *th* was unpronounceable. He tried hard to help us pronounce it correctly. "Place your tongue between your teeth and push air out your mouth. One, two, three: 'the.'" It was not pronounced correctly but resulted in a huge release of spit and a roar of hysterical laughter.

Another time, our zoology teacher came to class with a wet tomato in the pocket of his trousers. The poor man did not know why we were laughing until he reached into his pocket and withdrew a squashed tomato. It was rather sad, really, but we children found it awfully funny.

29
The Water Hole

I liked funny situations that lifted our spirits. Studying—learning new things—was important. Still, I did not like school very much. I loved to slip out of class, pretending a need to go to the bathroom, and then escaping to a stone ledge in the shade of an old fruit tree, where I liked to sit and enjoy the sounds and sights of nature. The serenity in nature was the world I loved best. It gave me joy and offset some of the chaos in our lives.

Playing hooky was not without peril. I knew I would pay a price. Still, being outdoors all alone was worth it. Some of the teachers got wise to my deceptions, however, and on reentering the classroom, I was frequently stopped before I got to my seat. Pointing to the blackboard, Pan (meaning Mister or Sir) Schreiber said, "Lusia, please illustrate the positive and negative charges in lightning." What did I care about positive and negative charges? I was embarrassed but gave a correct answer, although at other times, I did not. I had enough to worry about outside of school.

My mother was my constant worry. It was easy to crush her spirit. She was not strong enough, not like my father who seemed to overcome any obstacle. Mama was depressed at times. I worried about her health. I was terror stricken at the thought of her drowning in the water hole—the only source of our drinking water.

⁓

Our town had no piped-in water, no water wells, and no water pumps. The water flowed down the Pamir Mountains, the tallest mountain range on the border of Afghanistan to the south. From there, the water ran straight into Syr Darya, the river on the edge of town. The water somehow found its way into *arrik,* narrow ditches along the side of the wider alleyways. By the time the water reached the town and the arrik, it was usually polluted with debris. But as it was also used for irrigation, people fought for this water. In the middle of the night, neighbors redirected the water from each other's gardens. Next morning, huge brawls erupted everywhere. These fights often went beyond fistfights, often turning into armed conflicts with pitchforks or shovels used as weapons.

Eventually, the water reached the spot from which drinking water could be drawn. The access to this water hole was a slippery, wet bank without stairs or railing to hold on to. The surface of the water was covered in dead leaves, dead flies, and mosquitoes.

And sometimes, especially in the summer, Tajik teenage boys swam naked in the water hole. Often, when girls were seen near the water hole, naked teenagers would jump up above the surface, exposing themselves and laughing hysterically. In spite of these conditions, the water in the water hole remained our only water source. Its impurities and billions of organisms caused many infectious diseases. For that reason, this water had to be boiled.

Mama did not swim, and I believed that if I accompanied her to the water hole, I would save her from drowning. I also did not swim. I only felt secure when Papa brought the water home. He was a strong and skillful swimmer. But my mother's water expeditions remained my worst and never-ending fear. The water hole was my nemesis. It rarely gave me peace.

30
Tovarish Stalin—Russia Earth

Although we went to a Polish-speaking school, we were indoctrinated in Soviet thinking and steeped in Soviet patriotism. For the Soviets, the most important agenda was spreading propaganda. The truth had nothing to do with it. So we were constantly reminded of the highest authority of the land—Tovarish Stalin. We sang a popular song, thanking Tovarish Stalin for our *schaslivoye dyetstvo* (happy childhood). We were told to be thankful that all the food, clothing, and medicines went to the fighting men on the war's eastern front. It did not matter that we went without.

Posters on walls depicted brave Soviet soldiers slaying the evil dragons that represented Hitler and his Nazi troops. Over time, we grew to love—or pretended to love—Comrade Stalin and especially Mother Russia, our glorious land.

Papa was not political at all, and he was not very fond of Comrade Stalin or Communism. Given the circumstances in which he found himself, he grew suspicious, not trusting— especially of people he didn't know. He cared for his own family deeply. And although he loved Judaism, he exhibited signs of losing faith in God. He rarely said that "God will provide" anymore. He trusted his own instincts instead. Our survival and providing what meager bits of food he could gather amounted to his daily struggle.

Papa refused to accept the Soviet citizenship that was offered to us. He believed that if we were to become Soviet citizens, we would never be able to leave that country, not even after the war. He distrusted Soviet politics and Soviet politicians. Whenever anyone mentioned the NKVD, Papa put his finger to his mouth, signaling that we should speak in whispers. "You never know who may be listening," he would say.

But he did greatly admire Marshal Gregory Zhukov, the chief of the armed forces. The Russian people in general considered Zhukov the greatest war hero—and for good reason. He had defended Leningrad during the long siege from the beginning in 1941 throughout the entire year of 1942. In 1942, Zhukov also commanded the battle for Stalingrad that would prove the turning point of the war.

"Those Nazis, you just wait and see," my father would say. "Zhukov will clobber them to kingdom come and chase them all the way back to Berlin." He tried to keep track of the progress of war. Every so often, we listened to the latest news, *Poslednyi Chas*, on the loudspeaker in the center of town. No one knew for certain if the war reports we listened to were accurate or not. We did not have a choice of stations or our own radio to listen to.

There was a map of Europe hanging on the wall of our hut. Each time the Nazis retreated, Papa joyfully moved his little pins to the new positions. When things were not going well, he hardly glanced at his map. But, oh, how he cheered when the Nazis were defeated in battles on the eastern or western fronts. It was during the bloody battle for Stalingrad that Papa predicted Hitler's defeat.

People of the Soviet Union loved America and its people. Even before the United States entered the war, America regularly shipped battle tanks, rifles and other weapons, food, medicines, clothes, and more to support the Soviet war effort. It was all part of the Lend-Lease program initiated by President Franklin Delano Roosevelt as a way to help the Allied forces without actually entering the war. But the Russian people understood that with the help of the United States, the war against the Nazis could be won.

Most of us children understood the reasons for the deprivations we suffered. We were constantly reminded that each and every one of us needed to make sacrifices for the sake of the fighting men on the eastern front, for Mother Russia and the Russian Revolution of 1917.

It was 1944, and I was nearly eleven when our school was notified of the urgency of children making a contribution to the war effort. As soon as the school let out for the summer vacation, we were all conscripted for cotton picking.

Every morning, we were driven in trucks to the cotton fields. We picked cotton all day long, just so the fighting soldiers on the eastern front could stay warm all winter long in their padded cotton jackets. We worked hard. "Give 200 percent," we were told. We sang *"Za Rodinu, Za Stalina"*—200 percent for our nation and for Stalin. Sore and bloody fingers seemed like a small sacrifice for the war effort. Now, as I think back, it seems sad to have lost the lazy days of summer for the drudgery of cotton picking.

My least favorite summer job for Tovarish Stalin, Mother Russia, and the Russian Revolution was tending to the silkworms in their smelly cages. I remember it as if it were yesterday. Silkworms weave silk by nature, creating small cocoons the size of a tiny pinkie finger or half a pinkie. But they do it all—including mating and dirtying the cages.

As little as I was, I had a hard time bending down to reach the cages. It was tight in there, smelly, and so difficult to clean the cages and do whatever else needed to be done for the silkworms. The light was dim. There were no windows in the entire compound. The air was thick enough to cut with a knife. I hated the silkworms.

Sometimes, I gave myself permission for a good cry. It filled my heart with plenty of self-pity—an emotion frowned upon by some groups of people. I didn't care. Self-pity felt good. It was like being cleansed by the waves of an ocean. Most likely, it was really a cry of frustration, anger, maybe even defiance. Maybe I needed a shoulder to cry on. Mama didn't seem to understand—not because she didn't care about me but because she seemed to have lost hope for the future. I craved a smile or a sparkle in her eyes. It wasn't there.

At times like that, I remained near her, neither of us speaking. Speaking was pointless. I knew she loved me. She expressed it in a million different ways.

Love was different in the Soviet Union in those days of war. You hardly ever heard people verbally expressing love. The words alone didn't mean much and didn't help much. What was important and vital for survival was having people who cared deeply.

Throughout the war, six long years, we heard nothing from our family back home in Nazi-occupied Poland. The information on Soviet newscasts was selectively filtered. Nothing pertaining to the destruction of the European Jews reached the general population.

We spoke with longing of returning home to Poland and being reunited with our entire family. We spoke of the events we would recall, how we would celebrate our reunion after the war.

31
"I'm Not Hungry at All"

"I'm not hungry at all," Mama often said.

Mama made a practice of visiting the local bazaar walkways late in the afternoons, when the peddlers were getting ready to close shop. Sometimes, she picked up discarded, half-rotten fruit and vegetables. With the bad parts cut away, the fruit and vegetables tasted good. She checked for small, perfect, round holes in the fruit where the worms entered on their way to the core. We learned to eat a fruit, even if a worm lived inside. You simply bit off a piece and checked carefully. And if the rest of the fruit looked good, you took another bite. If not, you spit it out.

Lusia, Leninabad, Tajikistan

Mama worried about malnutrition; she believed it would stunt our growth. One time, she cooked soup from discarded radish leaves. The soup tasted so good. I asked for seconds. But the pot was empty, and Mama, so distraught, sat down and began to cry. I couldn't understand why she cried over an empty pot.

I don't recall having had eggs or meat throughout the entire war. We rarely had milk. They did sell horse meat in the bazaar—probably from horses that had died from hard labor or disease. Good thing we didn't have the rubles to buy it with. If we did, we would have eaten horse meat.

On very good days when Papa began earning some rubles by working with Abram, we ate soup cooked with lamb or beef bones. In addition to meat bones, the vendors sold kefir, the fermented milk drink of the region. On good days, we had kefir, our ration of bread, and tea for breakfast. Making tea was a process in itself. Some days, especially early in the morning when our stove remained unlit, Mama placed bits of dry tea into our old, chipped, enamel teapot, and one of us, either Frydzia or I, walked several streets over to the local *chayhanna*, the teahouse. For several kopecks, they poured *kepiatok,* boiled water, from a huge samovar into our teapot. And by the time we reached home, the tea was ready to be served.

Sometimes, Mama offered us her own ration of bread, always saying, "I'm not hungry at all." I believed it to be true because, most of the time, I accepted her bread. I wanted it to be true. How else could I eat her bread?

There was a baking oven in our courtyard as well. It was strange looking, round on the inside and out. On those rare occasions when our neighbor Rachel and her older daughter, Sara, baked the flat round bread, I made sure to hang around.

Not only was it interesting to watch the process as they slapped the round, flat dough against the inside walls of the hot oven, but best of all, I knew that I would surely receive a piece of the heavenly, hot, steaming, aroma-filled lepioshka—the dream of all dreams.

Like most children living in dire need of most necessities and all luxuries, I knew how to manipulate others for my own gain.

Early in the war, I learned how to scrounge around for food. I knew that if I hung around the busy market walkways and looked into the peddlers' eyes long enough, I would be rewarded with some almonds and some kind of dried fruit. Having blue eyes helped. Blue eyes were rare in central Asia. I am not sure if they liked my eyes, but they seemed fascinated, and it worked in my favor.

On hot summer nights, we slept in our courtyard—most of the time under special netting borrowed from our neighbors. The gentle breezes made the outdoor sleeping heavenly. The effect of the bright stars and the moon in the dark sky seemed too beautiful to be real. The sky seemed flooded with millions of stars, suspended in a silver net midway between earth and heaven. And during the full moon, everything seemed illuminated in bright light.

It was then that I learned about the constellations. I learned that these bright stars shone on the entire world. It was a wonder to me that the same stars cast their brilliant light on my home in faraway Poland. Home in Poland was never far from my thoughts.

The courtyard was securely bolted at night, so we felt safe from intruders. Still, we needed to protect ourselves from the inner courtyard intruders—strange flying or crawling creatures. Getting stung by a scorpion was no fun; I know because it happened to me.

It happened in daylight on a bright, sunny day. My screams brought out all our neighbors. Abram chased the scorpion, by then without its stinger. He caught the scorpion and placed it in a jar filled with some awful solution. It turned into a vile-smelling concoction that he applied to my foot. I have no idea why it worked, but my red and swollen foot felt better almost immediately.

I have no idea how we would have survived without our neighbors. Still, in spite of their help, our lives were in almost constant peril.

32
Purple Dye

Papa began dealing in an illegal business, buying and selling dye in its purest form. The dye came in the form of colored crystals. The process of packing this stuff was fascinating. Papa sat quietly at the table, preparing individual brown paper packages of dye. We were not allowed to speak or make unnecessary movements near the table.

The colored crystals were so potent that, during the process of wrapping the packages, even while breathing normally, Papa's face, especially around the nose and mouth, quickly became stained purple, red, green, or whatever color he was working with. He looked funny, but we were not allowed to laugh for fear of the dye staining him even more. Covering our mouths with our hands, we tried hard to conceal and silence our laughter.

To this day, I don't know where the dye originated from, but I suspect that Papa purchased this potent stuff from people who had stolen it from a government source. My father knew the risks involved. He carried the brown paper packages to the silk weavers, at some secret location, usually at night.

One night, he failed to come home. It was probably the most terrifying night of our lives. He was caught carrying the illegal stuff and was taken to the police station. There, he was charged with being *vrag naroda,* an enemy of the people, and the most serious charge of all—conspiring against the Russian Revolution! These charges were used arbitrarily against anyone for any crime, real or fictitious. Any minor wrongdoing could be twisted into a major offense of treason. My father spent a bad night, during which he was mistreated by the authorities, until Abram showed up next morning. Abram bribed the official, who duly looked the other way when Papa, accompanied by Abram, walked out of the jail.

Still, the stress in our lives increased dramatically. We had to find another way to deal with the crystal dye. Papa was now known to the police officials, but Mama, Frydzia, and I were not. So Mama started carrying the packages, with Papa following her at a distance. Soon, Frydzia and I took on the messenger job, with my father always following at a certain distance.

One time, on the way to a designated rendezvous, walking slowly and clutching the package tightly in my arms, I tripped and fell forward. That was probably the scariest moment of my life. I still remember that the dye I was carrying was purple. I was terrified that the brown paper package had broken wide open and that I was covered in purple. *Please God*, I prayed as I picked myself up. *Don't let me be purple. Please don't let me be purple.*

Quickly, I wiped my face with one free hand. No, there was no purple on my face. For a moment I felt relieved, but I could not turn around to look for my father. I did not dare. On those errands, he and I were not related.

I felt bad for him, knowing that he felt bad for me. Papa was a doer. He was very unhappy when he could not help out or do something good for his family. He was steps away from me, yet he could not help me. Purple has loomed large in my mind ever since that night.

Dangerous as it was to deal in these illegal dye transactions, it was all Papa could do to gain money, and doing it meant that hunger was no longer part of our lives. But the delivery errands had other dangers as well, as Mama and I found one evening that I remember clearly.

It was a Friday, the Muslim Sabbath. A powerful voice from high up in the minaret called the faithful to evening prayers. Mama and I set out just before nightfall to make the delivery. It was late when we were returning home. Tajik men dressed in their Friday best were leaving the mosque. The town was almost deserted as we got closer to our hut. I hated the dark and quiet streets. Where could you run from an attack inside those narrow streets? I felt uneasy, and I am sure Mama did too.

I don't know what made me turn around, but I did—and saw a Tajik man darting out of a doorway, running straight toward us. He grabbed my mother, and I screamed. He began beating her. I don't believe he was drunk. Muslims generally do not drink hard liquor. Yet there was such violence, such hatred, and savage passion in the way he beat her. Poor Mama screamed with pain, and I couldn't come to her rescue! Maybe it was fear of being hurt myself, but I seemed paralyzed, rooted to the spot. I just kept screaming, hoping someone would hear us and come to our rescue. No one did. Instead, the man eventually just stopped beating her, as if exhausted or no longer interested, and he simply walked off.

My mother managed to pull herself together. I remember her saying that he had knocked out her teeth and that she could not feel her face; it was numb. Fortunately, he had not actually knocked out her teeth, but Mama was sore all over her body, with bruises on her face, arms, and legs. She ached for weeks, and she was traumatized for longer than that. I knew because she spoke even less than normal. She just went about her chores. My father was quiet too. I have no idea what he felt—guilt possibly—because he had not been there to help or because he could not do the deliveries himself and thereby spare her from this danger. And, of course, he felt sadness, I am sure.

I often go back to that awful night. It has never totally left my consciousness. But my understanding of it has changed. When my mother was brutalized, I was very young, and I believed that my presence had saved my mother from being killed. Later, as I got older, I believed that my presence also saved my mother from being raped. Maybe that was partly true. Sometimes, I think there was another reason for the attack. Men routinely beat women in that part of the world. Sometimes, they even killed them, and the authorities turned a deaf ear to these incidents and to the plight of women in general. I remember hearing about a Tajik man who had killed his wife. "And he lives just a couple of streets from us," I heard my parents say.

Men in that culture believed that it was their right to punish women for the smallest infraction. Maybe my mother's attacker had seen her before and believed that she deserved to be punished for something. I think it is possible that my mother was brutalized because she dared to be seen in public in Western clothes, with her face and hair uncovered.

The stress and all the anxieties in my life caused me to act and think beyond my age. Emotionally and intellectually, I was maturing quickly. I began taking on new responsibilities for myself and my family.

Ironically, in school, we were routinely reminded that all was well, and we were well and happy to do everything we could for Tovarish Stalin *and* Mother Russia and the Russian Revolution.

33
End of War

The American president is dead; I remember well when I first heard those words. I was returning home from school one afternoon and walking in Madanyat Street near our hut when I overheard someone saying, "The American president is dead. President Roosevelt is dead."

President Roosevelt was frequently mentioned, especially when current events were discussed. In school, we studied only the most basics of the history of the United States and the most important presidents.

I understood even then and so far away from American shores that the United States had lost a great president. But in many ways, all Allied forces fighting the Nazis had also suffered a great loss. The Russian people considered President Roosevelt a great hero. I remember feeling very sad. Without the American president who would now help defeat the Nazis.

We spoke of the end of war with longing. "After the War" those were magical words. I remember a romantic song of the time about two people separated by war and how they promised each other to keep a rendezvous at a designated spot at exactly 6:00 p.m. after the war "when the lights go on again and the world is peaceful again"

For us, World War II ended May 10, 1945. That is when we first heard it. The news had reached us from other continents and thousands of miles away.

The Nazis had capitulated and had been defeated on western and eastern fronts. They had surrendered unconditionally. It was over. People rejoiced. Happiness overflowed in the tight and narrow alleyways of Leninabad. That same summer I had reached my twelfth birthday.

~

Yet, the spring of 1945 was not a good time for me personally. I contracted malaria, the dreaded disease of the region. My parents tried so hard to find quinine, the medicine which the visiting doctor promised would stop the awful chills and fever and sweating. I was fatigued most of the time, and the chills were excruciating.

One time, I remember clearly that it was middle of summer, and Mama had covered me with everything we owned---- blanket, even coats---and still the chills wouldn't stop. I asked Mama to hold me down physically, and then I pleaded with her to please lie down on top of me, anything to stop the shivering. Later Mama said we both shook from the chills! I didn't mind. I loved the tight embrace.

Eventually, Papa was able to purchase quinine in the black market. It stopped the chills but colored me yellow---my face, even the whites of my eyes and the rest of my body.

Malaria had taken a toll on my health. I had lost weight, my legs were like two sticks, and I had difficulty walking. The warm courtyard in front of our hut was my refuge and my favorite place. I spent many hours----days, in fact---under the mulberry tree that grew in our courtyard, reading books Frydzia brought from friends. I slept a lot. My family worried that sleeping long hours day and night might adversely affect my brain functioning. Still, it must have been the long rest---and the quinine---that helped me to recover from the awful disease. Slowly and very cautiously, I began to venture out of the courtyard.

Whenever I think back of that difficult summer of my malaria, I think of the mulberry tree and how much I loved it. Its branches hung low over the hut, and the mulberries covered the ground. If you did not step on them, you popped them straight into your mouth. Sometimes, we climbed into the tree and ate the berries directly from the branches, but not the summer of 1945. Not me; I lacked the strength to climb up into the branches. I just watched Frydzia sitting up there and filling our cooking pot full of berries. I watched her popping the berries into her mouth and sometimes tease me by showering me with a fistful of mulberries.

Those were happy times in our courtyard under the mulberry tree. I don't recall eating any mulberries off a tree in the good old days, before the war, back home in Poland. But the mulberries in our courtyard in Leninabad tasted great, and I never once got sick from eating them.

My bare feet were stained purple from the berries. I walked barefoot a lot, especially in the summer. Sometimes, my feet felt burning hot from the heat of the dirt streets. Often, I walked hugging the walls searching for a few inches of shade where the ground felt cooler. Still, I loved the freedom of bare feet. For the most part, life was better in the summer. Summer was good for chasing hunger away.

34
Summer of 1946

It was more than a year after the war had ended that our family and perhaps a dozen other families originally from Poland still remained in Leninabad.

We had been refused permits to travel back home to Poland and were referred to as "those people without a citizenship"— *bezgrazdanskye* in Russian. Papa had rejected Soviet citizenship in the belief that if we retained Polish citizenship, we would be able to go back home eventually. But he was always apprehensive about having made that decision. Still, he hoped in the end it would all work out in our favor.

But the Soviet system was not a democracy with freedom of choice and freedom of movement. Stalin was the law unto himself, the ultimate authority in the land. He could do anything he pleased against anyone, anytime.

The rumors that flew around suggested that we were being punished by Tovarish Stalin for rejecting Soviet citizenship. It was hard to believe, but according to those rumors, our punishment was that we would never go home again.

Our family and others like us were considered pariahs—very much like the Tartars, the Chechens, and the Ingush people who were deported deep into Kazakhstan and parts of Tajikistan from their native Crimea and Caucasus Mountains on the charge of collaborating with the Nazi German occupiers between 1941 and 1943.

Still, our only "sin" was the lack of Soviet citizenship. We didn't do anything wrong against the Soviet people, and we didn't deserve to be treated so badly. We huddled in our little hut with our worldly possessions packed in the ancient burlap flour sack, ready to go, hoping and believing that our travel permits would be granted soon.

School was out. Many school friends of ours and their families had already departed. The Jewish orphanage in Leninabad had disbanded, and our little cousins Syma and Frydzia and our friend Anita were among the orphaned children to leave next. So many people were allowed to go back—but not our family. Papa and Mama seemed depressed, and Frydzia and I felt lonely without our extended family and our friends.

There was nothing for us to do, so we took frequent trips to that part of Leninabad called "the new city" to visit the largest bazaar in town. Papa and Mama didn't like us moping around the house. They urged us to do something constructive.

So we started a little business of our own—turning cucumbers into pickles. We stuffed small cucumbers into a jar filled with water, small pieces of bread, and some salt and placed it in the hot sun. With the lid tightly closed, we created a fermentation tank that produced sour pickles within the span of one day.

We took the jar to the bazaar and positioned ourselves near other vendors. They were not too happy about our enterprise. They waved their hands at us angrily, as if to shoo us away, trying to discourage us from doing business in the bazaar. But people liked our pickles, and we did a brisk business. For a few kopecks a pickle, we emptied the jar very quickly. With our earnings, we bought fresh cucumbers and then ran home to start the whole process again.

Mama and Papa were proud of us. We helped supplement our daily existence, and that made us feel proud too.

But we also loved spending time in the bazaar among throngs of people. Some vendors were nice to us. Sometimes, they even offered us some dried fruit and almonds, especially when we looked at them with our big, sad eyes.

The atmosphere in our hut was not cheerful at all. Actually, it was quite depressing. Most everyone in our extended family had departed. First to go was Tante Bronia, and I missed her the most. She and Uncle Beno were "good citizens." They were well liked by the Soviets. Bronia had held a legitimate job working for Tovarish Stalin, the revolution, and Mother Russia. She was not a "speculant," as the Russians referred to people who engaged in illegal business, although the truth was that everyone who tried to survive did some illegal business on the side. To the Soviets, however, such people were counterrevolutionaries. And while it was true that Tante Bronia had a little job in the fruit processing factory turning uriuk apricots into preserves, it is also true that she was forced to steal jars of preserves just to supplement their daily existence. She sold the preserves and bought bread for herself and Uncle Beno. And these transactions generally took place in the black market. The Soviets believed Tante Bronia was a good citizen only because she was never caught stealing the fruit preserves.

Next to go was Tante Esther, Papa's oldest sister, and her husband, Uncle Benjamin the older, along with their youngest daughter, Tosia, their oldest daughter, Bella, and Bella's daughter, Lily. Lily was no longer a baby; she was six years old.

So many people were allowed to depart—but not us. We kept waiting, hoping to hear good news from the authorities. Almost daily, Papa visited the emigration office, inquiring about our travel permits. Each day, he came back disappointed—no travel permits.

Then one day in June, Papa returned home, his face transformed, exuding joy. He was absolutely glowing. I knew immediately that he had good news.

"We can go. We can leave today. Do you hear me? We can go!" His voice rose, and in his hands, he waved a sheet of paper over our heads. Mama, Frydzia, and I just stood there in disbelief. Then I ran up to him, trying to grab the paper in his hand. He wouldn't let go. "No," he said, "let me read it to you."

It was just a few words on a piece of paper, but it said volumes. It changed our lives. I will never forget that paper and those few words—"permission to depart from Leninabad ..."

Within minutes, we had gathered up our meager belongings; our home was once again transformed into a hut with four empty walls. We said good-bye to our dear neighbors, Rachel, her daughters, Sara and Zina, and son, Abram; all had tears in their eyes. "One day we will meet again," they intoned. They too were hoping to leave the Soviet Union.

With our bundles in our hands, we ran all the way to the station on the outskirts of Leninabad. In the station, we ran into a few families we had known for years. They too had received permission to depart Leninabad. We piled into a cattle train—only this time, the boxcars were no reason to despair but to rejoice and celebrate. At last, we were going home.

35
Coming Home

It was a long trip. It took weeks in those days to go from Asia to Europe. At first, the unvarying, windy steppes of Kazakhstan out the train window made for long, boring days across hundreds and hundreds of miles—no one knew for sure how many. Still, we were happy.

We were going home—there to be reunited with family we had not seen in six years. Papa and Mama spoke with great anticipation of being reunited with their sisters and brothers after all those difficult six years of war.

We arrived in Poland six weeks after leaving Leninabad. It was still summer, so different here from the scorching summer of central Asia. Unlike Leninabad, the Polish summer offered an abundance of flowers.

Finally, we came home to Poland. What was to have been the best time of our lives turned out to be the worst possible time of our lives. This was not the same Poland we had fled six years earlier. Something was terribly wrong in the country we had so longed to return to.

In some stations, we heard terrible comments from the local population.

"Look," I remember hearing someone say, "unslaughtered chickens are returning."

There were disquieting rumors—unbelievable rumors—of Jewish people having been slaughtered in ghettos and extermination camps, betrayed and denounced by their Polish neighbors. The price for handing over a Jew was half a kilo of sugar! And sometimes, Jews were handed over to the SS men or the Gestapo for nothing at all—no sugar or anything.

We had not heard such things before. How could they be true? We could not accept such a cruel reality. It was too horrible and too evil to comprehend.

We spent several weeks in Krakow that summer. We thought it was the best location to search for members of our family, and it was close to our home in Sucha.

We found no one alive. Mama's two sisters and two brothers, Papa's one sister and one brother, and dozens of family members on both sides had all been killed by the Nazis and their Polish and Ukrainian collaborators.

Later, we learned that, here and there, Polish people, called the Righteous Among the Nations, saved Jewish lives. Unfortunately, there weren't enough such good people.

During our stay in Krakow, which was only fifty miles north of Sucha, Papa contacted a Polish neighbor he knew before the war. The man warned him not to return to Sucha for the purpose of reclaiming our properties. It wasn't safe. He would be risking his life, he was told.

There were many incidents of Jewish survivors massacred in Poland shortly after the war, only because they dared to go back to their homes.

Before the war, there were about twenty-four thousand Jewish inhabitants in Kielce, a city in southeast Poland. Only two hundred survived the Holocaust. They returned to their homes, and some even were successful in reclaiming their properties. But the Polish people did not want the Jewish survivors to return to Kielce or anywhere in Poland.

In July 1946, one year after the war and only weeks before we returned to Poland, more than forty Jewish Kielce survivors were killed in an old-fashioned pogrom by Polish soldiers, police, and civilians. So we never went back home to Sucha.

Frydzia and I didn't quite understand the enormous tragedy that had occurred. I also don't believe our parents understood. Both walked around in a daze. They didn't sleep, they didn't eat; they hardly spoke. Papa had always been able to solve problems, big and small. His determination had helped him conquer most difficult situations—but not this one.

For the first time, I witnessed my father completely defeated. His moods kept changing—depressed and defeated one moment and then outraged and pouring forth angry words the next.

That summer, Papa learned that Uncle Mehul, his oldest brother who was like a father to him when he was little, had been shot by a Polish man in front of his synagogue in 1942. Papa vowed to find the man who killed his brother and kill him with his bare hands. Mama was terribly upset and tried to dissuade him. "Leave him to God," she kept saying. "He will be punished." This awful state of rage and depression lasted through the rest of the summer.

There was a brief moment of enjoyment that summer when we were reunited with our extended family that had departed Leninabad prior to our departure. They had settled in a town called Dzierzoniow in the western part of Poland. So we were together, all of us again, and that gave us some comfort. I especially remember the tranquility of Sabbath afternoons together with Tante Esther and Tante Bronia, our uncles, and our cousins.

The last communication (a postcard) from Papa's brother Mehul in Nazi-occupied Poland that reached the family in Siberia

One day, as if he were waking up from a vegetative state, a much-less-angry Papa announced, "We have to leave. We cannot remain in this country. This land is drenched in the blood of our people."

So we were off again, on a journey to nowhere, just away. The following months, we covered hundreds of miles, crossing borders illegally. We crossed the Polish border into Bratislava, Czechoslovakia, wading in the shallow waters of a river separating the two countries.

In our wet clothes, we searched unsuccessfully for some shelter. Papa found someone willing to smuggle us across yet another border, this time into Austria. In the middle of the night, we piled into a truck. To conceal the cargo he was transporting, the driver threw a huge canvas sheet over all four of us. We traveled all night, asleep under the canvas sheet. I don't recall waking even once.

We arrived in Vienna early the next morning. I had never been to Vienna before, but my parents had always spoken of it as a beautiful city.

Well, it was not a beautiful city anymore. It was completely bombed out. Destroyed buildings stood like skeletons, their roofs gone, their windows shattered. Piles of debris littered streets and sidewalks. Vienna appeared devoid of all human presence, as if everyone had departed the once beautiful city. It seemed dead.

Vienna was divided into four zones: American, British, French, and Soviet. Papa asked the driver to take us to the part of Vienna occupied by the American troops. The driver hesitated; he thought we would all get into trouble if we tried to enter the American zone. We pleaded with him to please take us there. Finally, he agreed.

This was our first encounter with American people. In spite of the language barrier, I noted the calmness about the American soldiers, so different from other soldiers I had encountered in my early childhood. The American soldiers seemed so relaxed, moving slowly, even speaking slowly, almost stretching each word beyond anything I had heard before.

Although I couldn't understand most of what was said, I felt no fear of the American soldiers. It was amazing to me that people of such courage and bravery in winning a war seemed so easygoing, so relaxed, even smiling. Who smiled in those days? Only the Americans did!

We were offered temporary shelter in a huge building, the Rothschild Hospital, one of the few structures not completely destroyed during the war. The Rothschild Hospital was built in the late nineteenth century by Anselm von Rothschild for patients with neurological illnesses. After the war, it was transformed into a shelter mostly for homeless Jewish survivors like us.

For the first time in a very long time, we were going to sleep in our own individual canvas cots with our own pillows and the standard US green army blankets; we were also given a food ration, but before receiving it, we were required to undergo fumigation against lice.

The American army personnel were very polite and seemed understanding of people's reluctance to be sprayed. Here and there, in fact, some people were so upset that they were crying. The fumigation didn't frighten me, although all four of us looked very odd; our faces, our hair, and our clothes were all white with the strange powder.

We remained in the hospital for several days. It was a fine place for a good rest. We liked the American army food rations— canned meat that tasted salty but good. Even my kosher parents enjoyed eating the American canned meat; we all did. Our cots were especially wonderful, real luxury after the crowded and uncomfortable sleeping conditions during the war. But we were being encouraged to move on, perhaps to relocate to displaced persons camps in other parts of Austria or Germany. Ironically, that was our next and last stop—Germany.

Again, we were given temporary lodging. Everything was temporary in our lives, until such time as we too would have a home of our own.

This time, the temporary lodging was a displaced persons camp in Traunstein, a small town near Munich, Germany—the first DP camp of many to follow.

In Traunstein, we were reunited with Tante Bronia and Uncle Beno—it was a happy day for all of us. I was deliriously happy to have my Bronia all to myself. The rest of our extended family had left Poland as well, hoping to reach the shores of Palestine that were eventually to become Israel. Tante Bronia and Uncle Beno also hoped to go to Palestine.

Although my greatest wish was to live in Palestine—which would later become a Jewish state for the first time in two millennia—my parents felt that, after all those long and bitter years of war, we needed a safe haven. And that was America.

36
More Homelessness

Winter that year of 1946/47 was cold and gloomy. Snow was piled high. I used to stand at the window in the large, communal dormitory, observing people below, watching them trudging slowly in the snow toward the communal kitchen with pots in their hands, coming and going.

You could tell whether the little utensils were full or empty by the way they were held. Sometimes, the pot was held close to the body, perhaps to keep the person warm. It was a sad scene. *When will all this end?* I wondered. *When will these people—and we too—have a normal life?*

Well, never mind—I didn't even know what a normal life was anymore. In many ways, this was normal for me. I was just a thirteen-year-old girl. I had not been to school in more than one year. I didn't have any friends. You can't have friends when you're on the go constantly. *But maybe one day I will have a friend*, I thought. In the meantime, Frydzia was my friend.

We discussed all kinds of things we couldn't share with Mama and Papa. Besides, they worried so much about us. I knew they wanted to give us a better life—not this communal life, with living quarters the size of a canvas cot. Sometimes, the cots were surrounded by cloth sheets fastened to the ceiling.

I knew a little about what went on behind the sheets ... but I didn't like hearing such sounds in the middle of the night.

37
Saying Good-Bye Again

It seemed like winter would never end, and 1946 turned to 1947.

One day in February, Papa said he had something important to tell my sister and me. Mama just sat there looking unhappy, as if she knew something we didn't. I saw pain in her eyes and braced myself for something I had always hated—a surprise. I was always afraid of changes in our lives. I wanted everything to remain as it was, as long as we could all be together.

Papa's face wore a serious look—not a good sign. For a moment, he just looked at Frydzia and me, not saying anything. Then he spoke.

"We've been living in this hole, and I see no way out," he began. "This is not a life for two young girls. There has to be a better place.

"Someone will take you across the border to Belgium. There is a place for orphaned Jewish children who survived the war. You will have enough food. You will go to school. You will live a normal life. And soon, we will be reunited, maybe in a couple of months, maybe half a year at most."

I cannot listen to this, I thought. *It is too painful.* I needed to be home—wherever home happened to be. I needed to be near Mama and Papa. Instead, they were sending us away. I felt as if I were being banished.

Saying good-bye to Mama and Papa was so painful. We boarded a train. With my face glued to the windowpane, I needed to keep them in my vision for as long as I could, until they became a mere speck in the distance. Then they disappeared. Frydzia and I sat down across from one another, crying.

Out the window, I saw tiny cottages, the rooftops covered in snow, and white clouds of smoke escaping from the chimneys. It was strange how warm those homes appeared, even under a cover of snow.

I needed to use the bathroom. It was at the other end of the car. It was cold in there and drafty, and the train shook and rumbled. I couldn't stay seated on the toilet. I looked down, and there was blood on my bare thighs. *What is that—what is happening?* I thought in a kind of panic. I stood up and looked down my legs as a flow of blood coursed down to the top edge of my kneesocks.

I began to realize what had happened, but why now on this train? I needed so badly to be home with Mama.

To stop the bleeding, I stuffed rough toilet paper into my underwear. It felt like newspaper against my legs. I wiped my legs with more paper and pulled my kneesocks as high as they would go. Then I went back to the compartment.

Why was Frydzia staring at me like that? Was it the way I walked, or was it that I carried with me a huge supply of toilet paper? I told her what had happened. She didn't say much and just drew me close to her. "You'll be fine," she said.

We arrived in Cologne, a major city in the western part of Germany, near the Belgian border. I could no longer keep track of all the borders we had crossed illegally. Papa told us Cologne would be our last stop.

"Someone will be waiting for you," he had assured us. We got off the train. It was late, and it was dark. We were tired and finished with crying.

We stood quietly on the platform, not knowing what to do or whom to look for. A man was staring at us. He walked over and greeted us in German. "*Guten abend*," he said. Good evening. Then he told us to follow him.

He took us to an old, beat-up car and told us to sit in the back. We followed his instructions. The man never introduced himself. He drove us to the edge of a forest, dropped us off, and told us to wait for him. He said nothing else. We were like two marionettes. We did as we were told. I was wary and a little scared of the stranger. I didn't trust him. Frydzia stared at me. I think she was frightened too.

The man returned, and we followed him into the dark forest. We stopped before a wooden cottage. He motioned us inside. The cottage seemed even darker than the dense woods. The man walked over to a table in the corner of the room and struck a match. He lit the wick under a glass chimney of a kerosene lamp.

Slowly, I grew accustomed to the dimness of the large room and the woodsy scent around us. Then I saw a large, stone fireplace. I moved a little closer, searching for warmth from a fireplace that was barely lit but nevertheless felt warm.

The man motioned us to sit opposite the fireplace. He didn't say much. His appearance struck me as sinister; he was scary looking. We didn't speak, and we didn't take our eyes off him. We watched his every move. He poked logs in the fireplace, and the fire seemed to come alive. Tiny flames escaped from the pit underneath and licked the logs. The stranger sat down opposite us, so close I could see every muscle in his face and the tension in his eyes. There was tension in the air too, a sense of utmost gravity. I felt as if something might happen any moment.

He began to speak, something about crossing a border illegally and the dangers in doing so. I was not afraid of the border crossing; I was used to that illegal activity. I was afraid of the stranger.

"At the crossing of the border, there will be a ravine separating Germany from Belgium," he said. He went on and on about the seriousness of the illegal crossing. I wondered if Papa had paid this man to take us across to Belgium. Had Papa met him personally? Did he trust him? Could we trust him?

"Soon, we will go deeper into the forest," he said, "but the best time to depart is shortly after midnight. Maybe the patrol guards will be dozing off, but we have to watch out for the dogs."

Now, I was really afraid. I pictured huge fangs and saliva drooling out of the dogs' angry, grinning mouths.

Before we set out on the most important part of our journey, Frydzia asked our stranger if we could use the bathroom. He opened the door of the cottage and pointed to the rear part of the grounds where the outhouse stood. It was dark and scary in there, so we relieved ourselves in the back of the cottage.

We crossed a narrow path at the far end of the property.

There were no stars and no moon in the little bit of sky I could see in the middle of the dense forest. The darkness was eerie but protective. We walked quietly, trying hard not to make a sound. The ground was covered in patches of snow, mixed with layers upon layers of dead leaves and pieces of dead wood. It was hard to find level ground to walk on in that darkness. The sounds were like thunder as we tumbled over fallen logs. With my bare hands, I felt for the rotted tree stumps.

Every so often, the man stopped to listen or to reorient himself. He communicated in gestures—a hand held up told us to stop; a finger over his mouth was a sign not to speak.

The forest grew even thicker, and there was lots of mud under our feet. Some tree branches and low-growing shrubs made walking even more difficult. My coat got caught on some branches that trailed all the way down to the ground. I lost my hat somewhere, and my scarf was a nuisance, snagging everything along the way. I used my hands constantly to push the brush away. My hands and my face felt sore.

I couldn't see anything, but I felt the space around me. The forest was filled with a life that made its own undisturbed sounds. The life of the forest could make sounds, but we had to remain very quiet.

I walked into a shrub. It scratched my face. My face felt sore and wet. My hair was wet. My coat, my legs, and my shoes were wet and covered in mud.

I felt so tired. I would have liked to take a rest, but I knew I couldn't do that; now was not the time. There was so much walking. It seemed so long, hours, since we had left the cottage.

Then I saw a light in the distance. Was the dawn breaking— or was it a light from the other side of the border, across the ravine the man had described to us back in the hut? If so, we were close to the border, the guards, and the dogs, and that meant we had to be even more careful.

Suddenly, I felt someone grab my arm. I thought someone was holding Frydzia. *We've been caught! This is the end of our journey.* Then I glanced to my right to get a better look and saw only our stranger. It was he who was holding us. I stopped being afraid of him, recognizing he meant us no harm. He let go of us and pointed toward the light and the ravine.

"Now is the moment," he whispered to us. "You must run fast. Run past the ravine. Don't stop for anything, not the guards, not the dogs. Just keep on running. Past the ravine you will be in Belgium. Once there, find a train station. Get on the train till you get to Brussels. Now, run! Run! God be with you!"

38
A Beautiful Lady

We ran and ran, and no one stopped us—not the guards, not the dogs, no one. We felt exhausted. We had run past the ravine, and we sat down at the side of the road. It was no longer dark. It was daylight, and everything looked different. Everything seemed better.

We decided to rest before finding a train station and almost instantly drifted off into a sound sleep, only to be awakened by a stranger. He spoke French and then German. He seemed truly concerned about us sleeping on the side of the road. "Are you all right? Where do you live? Do you need anything?" he asked. We felt so tired that all we could do was shake our heads.

I don't recall finding the train station or what it looked like. And I only vaguely recall getting on the train. We had not eaten for many hours, but I don't recall feeling hungry. We had no tickets, yet we were not refused seats on the train. I felt such total exhaustion. We felt completely drained as we stretched out, both of us across several seats. No one seemed to mind; on the contrary, people gave us ample space. I think they were shocked to see the condition we were in. We were disheveled, covered in mud. I remember that some passengers stared at us, and some pretended not to look.

As tired as I felt, I remember thinking that the other passengers seemed well dressed and looked healthier, almost prosperous, as if they had not suffered any deprivations of war, as if there had been no war. I couldn't help noticing that Belgium was more normal than other countries we had been to.

I have no recollection of the train ride to Brussels until someone shook us awake.

"It's your stop. This is Brussels. You need to change trains here for Antwerp."

I have no recollection of finally arriving in Antwerp, but I knew we had come to the right place—Papa had scribbled the address on two pieces of paper and placed each one of them inside our coat pockets.

The building appeared small from the outside, a townhouse facade attached on both sides. But inside, the space was enormous. Although it was an orphanage, it felt homey with a relaxed air about it.

Boys and girls of all ages—some as young as four years old—who were rescued by Christian families or hidden in churches and convents during the war were now running, playing, and laughing. Some were reading. The older ones were interacting with the little ones—helping with their homework, I assumed.

We were instructed to sit on a wooden bench out in the entry hall. Again, we felt stared at. They also pretended not to look, but I knew they were all stealing glances at us.

Moments later, in came a man and a woman, both perhaps in their fifties. Later, I learned that both were directors of the facility. Then a beautiful young woman in a white uniform and wearing a white cap joined them. All three looked at us with disbelief in their eyes. They seemed to be figuratively scratching their heads, not knowing exactly what to do with us.

They spoke in whispers—I'm sure to spare us embarrassment—occasionally glancing at us as if that would give them a clue. I have no doubt that our appearance screamed the need for urgent care. But I was beyond feeling anything—and beyond caring what people thought. I just wanted to sleep. It was obvious that these three adults were trying to solve a problem and come up with a plan for us.

I thought I overheard them discussing our clothes. I knew we appeared dirty and disheveled, but I didn't expect never to see my clothes again. In fact, that is exactly what happened: everything we wore was discarded immediately.

The young woman in white asked us to follow her. She smiled, and I could not take my eyes off her beautiful smile. I guess I always liked it when people smiled.

We climbed a flight of stairs leading to a long corridor lined with many doors on each side. She told my sister to remain in the corridor and wait for her. I didn't know what to make of it. Over the years, I had grown to suspect every intention toward my family—good and bad. And now, Frydzia and I were being separated for the first time.

The young woman opened a door to what looked like a bathroom. I saw a sight I had not seen in years—maybe never—a room for bathing and cleaning up. I knew such rooms existed, but I could not recall having experienced one firsthand. The tiles on the floor were black and white, and the walls were white. The tub was already filled with warm water. The entire room seemed veiled in warm mist—it felt heavenly. This wasn't real. So many first experiences. I just stood there transfixed and tired.

"You should get undressed now," the woman in white said, "and place all your clothes in the hamper back there in the corner and then get into the warm tub."

She handed me a bar of soap and told me to take as long as I wished. All that kindness, and I doubted even genuine and honest intentions. It was all so overwhelming. With a smile on her face, she turned and gently closed the door behind her.

In all my thirteen years, I couldn't recall ever being in a room by myself with a closed door. It felt strange. The tranquility of the room and the stillness of the moist air made for an almost out-of-body experience. Instead of getting washed, I just sat on a stool and looked around. Then I remembered the tub and the warm water. I tried to remember when or if I had ever bathed in a tub of warm water. In the camps, we used to shower in communal showers under huge, flat showerheads suspended from the ceiling—but a tub of warm water for me alone? I could not remember such a thing ever happening.

Getting clean was no small effort, especially my hair, now a tangled mass, barely resembling my long, thick brown hair. I scrubbed and scrubbed until I ached all over. I saw dirt floating on the surface of the water. I was horrified. I stood up and reached for a long hose. With much turning and twisting I finally got a powerful jet of water to spill out of the hose. I rinsed my hair and the rest of my body and let the filthy water drain out.

I stepped out of the tub and walked over to the hamper for a last look at my clothes. I just stood there, dripping wet. Nothing belonged to me. It felt good. I felt free. Finally, I had scrubbed away all the grime and dirt of all those nasty years of war. Watching the dirty water running down the drain was a promise of something good.

I heard a knock on the door. The beautiful lady in white stepped in holding a large white sheet. I worried about the remaining dirty water in the tub. I hoped she had not noticed. She just stood there for a short moment looking at me and then quickly draped the sheet around me and drew me close to her. I thought I saw tears in her eyes.

That evening, Frydzia and I were indeed separated for the first time. After having had some bread and a glass of milk, I was led to a room that appeared like a large dormitory. Actually, it was one of four dormitory rooms in the home. It was lined with many beds on both sides.

This was a room for the youngest girls, between the ages of four and thirteen. I was among the oldest. At first, I cried. Why was my sister taken away from me? I couldn't understand. I needed to be among the oldest girls, not the youngest. Was I expected to give something of myself to these little children? I was tired in so many ways. I had nothing to give anymore. I wanted others to give to me. I needed desperately for someone to look after me.

That night, I went to sleep in my own bed—not a canvas cot but a real bed with several blankets, a soft fluffy pillow inside a freshly laundered white pillowcase. I took such care not to disturb the beautifully made-up bed—I crawled on my hands and knees into what seemed like a haven of two white sheets. For the first time in my life, I went to sleep between two sheets! This was no dream, and it was no ordinary sleep. This really felt like I had died and went to heaven.

Next morning, I was awakened to a ruckus of little girls chattering, some asking to be helped with getting dressed and washing up.

Oostduinkerke, Belgian shore, Summer, 1946.
Orphaned Jewish children rescued by Christian families, Churches and Convents during World War II

39
Hilda—Mother Image

At breakfast, I was allowed to join the older girls, my sister among them, around a long table. And there was so much food. Mostly, I recall a huge platter of scrambled eggs and sliced bread with a thick spread of butter. Bread had always been my favorite food. But the half a grapefruit in front of each of us, I didn't know what to make of it or how to eat it. I had never seen it before. I just sat there staring at it.

Frydzia and I had been introduced to the cook the night before. Her name was Hilda, and she was rather large. But later, I learned she was large in so many good ways. Her heart was large. Sometimes, I wished she was my mother. I think I searched for a mother image during our entire stay in the Antwerp home. Hilda was watching me being puzzled by the grapefruit. She approached the table, grabbed my right hand still holding the spoon, and with her hand pushing on mine, we plunged into the grapefruit and it splashed my face. My first taste of the tangy fruit came from the juice that had been dripping down my face. Still, I came to love that woman. Hilda was German, and she was Jewish, and she was the first person we could communicate with because she spoke German, the language Frydzia and I understood.

Everyone else spoke Flemish or French. Frydzia and I experienced a language barrier. From the very start, the staff members tried hard to communicate with us through gestures and some Yiddish words. But they felt that learning French was extremely important, so we were enrolled in a French-speaking school almost immediately.

At first, it was difficult not being able to communicate with children my own age. I needed a friend, and I was anxious to make friends. All I could do was smile and nod my head. Still, I believed that soon I would be able to speak their language. Papa was right that life would be normal and that we would have plenty to eat. Still, there were moments every day when I missed my parents terribly.

Before long, I was asked by a staff member to help with the morning routine of getting a little girl ready for breakfast. We were introduced. Her name was Dora, and she was so sweet. Dora was six years old. She spoke French only and that was how she communicated with me. I felt embarrassed and confused, but I was eager to help Dora with the morning routine. At the same time, I was learning French from little Dora. It gave me a sense of accomplishment, and I was beginning to understand my place in the room for the youngest children. Perhaps the staff members believed that by helping the little girls I was helping myself to overcome my own emotional difficulties.

The little girls that ran around and played happy games and smiled during the day were in fact experiencing terrible nightmares each night and reliving their own traumatic early childhoods. Some remembered their mothers and fathers taken away by the Gestapo, and some were too young to remember anything, so it seemed. Still, they cried out in their sleep. It didn't take much for me to understand how lucky I was. I had Frydzia, and I had my parents!

Celebrating Chanukah, Antwerp, Belgium, 1947,
Lusia front row, second on the right

40
Survivors' Communication Board

For more than a year, we lived in the home for orphaned Holocaust children in Antwerp. Then Frydzia and I returned to a DP camp in Germany to be reunited with Mama and Papa. I didn't care that it was Germany. All I wanted was to be with them. I missed Mama and Papa tremendously. Papa kept in touch with his brother, our uncle Jack in Brooklyn, New York. Uncle Jack promised to bring us to America, however long it would take.

It was three years after the end of the war, and it was our fourth DP camp. So much had happened. My parents still lived under the sword of their tragic loss of their sisters and brothers, nieces and nephews, and cousins—literally, dozens of members on both sides of the family.

For my mother, one loss in particular weighed upon her and seemed to embody all the unspeakable grief of the Holocaust. It had its beginning long before on that night in October 1939, when we had encountered the stranger in white my mother always referred to as the "guiding angel," the man who had reached out of the darkness to save our lives.

Mama and Papa, DP camp in Germany

That cold, wet night, we had traveled all night long. First light found us at a small village, yet this tiny place was a hive of chaotic activity, and an uninterrupted hum of human voices emanated from the center of it.

Our coachman maneuvered the wagon into a spot at the edge of the village, and my parents told Frydzia and me to stay put in the wagon while they walked away to find out what was going on. As always, I felt frightened seeing my parents depart, but Frydzia held and squeezed my hand hard, giving me the reassurance I needed.

There, in the middle of the crowded main street filled with people and vehicles, an utterly amazing coincidence occurred; my mother ran into her oldest sister, Tante Hanah, and Hanah's nine-year-old daughter, my cousin Feige. They too were far from home on that fateful morning. Hanah's husband was at home in Brzesko, a town in southern Poland, with their two younger children. Hanah and Feige were trying to reach their home.

As Mama and Tante Hanah came toward our wagon, it seemed clear to me that they were discussing something important. Their gestures and their faces seemed agitated. Their bodies seemed to bend in despair. Both cried and wiped their eyes. It seemed a desperate situation that I did not understand.

Later that day, we said good-bye to Tante Hanah and Feige, and for years, we all assumed they were home and safe. Long afterward, I learned about the sisters' conversation. Hanah had begged Mama to take Feige on our journey, but Mama refused, saying she could not undertake such a responsibility and that, in times of great turmoil, "children should not be separated from parents."

Hanah, Feige, and the rest of their immediate family were killed in the Holocaust. To this day, I remember my cousin Feige—a tall, skinny girl with long brown curls. The death of my cousin Feige, her two little brothers, and all the little children embody the evil that was the Holocaust.

Mama lived a long life—she reached the age of 101! She spoke rarely about the loss of her family. But the weight of pain, tinged with guilt, stayed with her the rest of her life. "If only I had a picture," she would say sometimes. "I can't remember what they looked like."

For her and Papa, the agony of loss could be seen and felt in everything they did. Their daily activities had become almost mechanical; they performed them like a couple of robots, without thought or feeling. There was no joy in anything they did. And their depression was infectious, weighing heavily on our hearts.

They were not alone. Virtually everyone in the DP camps had suffered similar losses. We lived in an environment of deep depression and unspeakable tragedy.

My parents were photographed, I think, for an identification card to be used in the soup kitchen in the camp. It is probably the most sorrowful photograph I have ever seen—a middle-aged couple, thin and haggard looking, with deep-set eyes, absent and unseeing.

Sometimes, I saw a glimmer of hope, a spark of life in their eyes. This happened only when they read the names of survivors posted on a huge bulletin board in the community building. The long exterior wall was plastered with handwritten scraps of paper as well, a communication board of the most desperate kind—"I am looking for my brother ..." and "Has anyone seen ...?" On and on went these heartbreaking lists of names of mothers, fathers, siblings, husbands, and wives. Even three years after the war had ended, people kept on searching for loved ones, refusing to accept reality.

Always with a sliver of hope, Papa and Mama searched for familiar names. Maybe someone among the survivors would remember seeing a sister or brother in a camp or a ghetto. They checked the lists almost daily, and they posted their own notices. "Has anyone seen my sister Hava Urbach-Rand from Biala-Bielsko? Her sister Rosa survived the war and is hoping to find her." "Perhaps someone has seen my sister Hanah ... my brother Isaac ... my brother David ..." No one ever responded, and the dispirited expression in their eyes and body language came back to stay.

They also clearly felt survivors' guilt—especially my mother. "I don't understand," she would say. "Was I any better than Hanah or Hava? Did I give more *tzedaka* [charity] to the poor? How does God decide who is to live and who is to die?" She was so angry at God. I knew it, I felt it, and I saw it in her eyes.

Uncle Jack, Papa's brother in America, was trying all this time to take us out of this homeless existence. He regularly kept us informed about the process of securing affidavits for visas to enter the United States. The process was very slow, for American law still maintained a low quota for immigrants from the Eastern European countries. For that reason, Uncle Jack also traveled to Ottawa, Canada, to secure Canadian visas if the US visas did not materialize.

Mama, US immigration/affidavit photo,

Papa, US immigration/affidavit photo

41
To America

We heard that on June 25, 1948, the Eightieth Congress had passed a new law: the 1948 Displaced Persons Act authorizing the admission into the United States of certain European displaced persons for permanent residence. The new law specified that the individuals could bring their families with them as long as they were "good" citizens, who could stay out of jail and provide financially for themselves without public assistance.

The new law had revoked the old quota immigration system. Instead of a trickle of immigrants from Eastern Europe, the new law opened the gates to thousands of homeless people like us, living in camps like ours, across the European continent. President Harry Truman was instrumental in passing the new immigration legislation. He was our true hero.

So, with the sudden change in our immigration status and with Uncle Jack's efforts to get us to America, there was hope that it might actually happen—soon. We might finally be going to our new home.

Uncle Jack, our American uncle

I was too young to remember what a real home was like. It had been almost ten years since I had experienced a real home. What would it be like to have a home with more than one room? I couldn't even imagine that.

I had recently seen films made in Great Britain and America showing resplendent, palatial homes and beautiful ladies wearing beautiful ball gowns, descending grand marble stairs under magnificent crystal chandeliers. I didn't understand or even believe there was such a life. I preferred films portraying simple lives in homes with white picket fences. Most of all, I dreamed of a bathroom—a real home with a bathroom. The very thought was unbelievable.

In the camp, we all used a communal shower. Once a week, women of all ages and their young children flocked without fail to the shower—at either 6:00 p.m. or 8:00 p.m. Despite the lack of privacy, the shower was greatly appreciated and was looked forward to with much anticipation. Benches against the walls of the shower room ensured that, in addition to getting scrubbed, there would also be an opportunity for socializing and people watching.

I remember standing under the huge, flat showerheads suspended from the ceiling and the delightful feeling of being enveloped in the warm flow of water. I was young, and my body was developing. I was keenly aware of being looked at—in a nice way—but there were no full-length mirrors anywhere, so I could not see myself as others did. Perhaps this is why, when I dreamed of a real bathroom, my mind's eye saw it with a full-length mirror.

I was fifteen, approaching my sixteenth birthday, when we moved to a transit camp called Funk Kaserne outside of Munich, Germany. There, the US immigration officials put us through a battery of tests—physical exams, psychological exams, chest X-rays, and other lab tests.

What kind of results were they looking for? Did they really expect these remnant survivors of the Holocaust to be in good health? Could the immigration officials even comprehend the survivors' physical and mental scars?

We were scheduled for interrogation about our political affiliations as well. Based on rumors, we understood that the US immigration officials preferred if the prospective immigrants disliked the Communist ideology. But we had already experienced Communism firsthand. We lived under the Soviet totalitarian rule for six long years. And life was difficult under that system. Yet I recall Papa saying, "Don't say anything good about the Soviet Union. We don't want them to think we liked it there."

I was terribly frightened of being interviewed by three uniformed men, whose language I hardly understood. Perhaps one of the men was an interpreter, and perhaps they asked simple questions. Is it not strange that I cannot recall what questions were asked or recall the answers I gave? I only remember being fearful of saying the wrong thing. For me, it was like a test. Would I pass? Was I worthy of having a home in America, the land that one could only dream of?

But being healthy was one of the most important criteria. I do not know how many among us were really healthy, how many were completely sane, and who among us cared much about politics. What we all hoped for was a real home— someplace safe.

For the first physical exam, we felt both fearful and encouraged. We got there early, but to our surprise, so did everyone else, and hundreds of people milled about outside the administration building before it even opened its doors. When it did open, the officials couldn't keep the crowds back. People stormed the building—completely out of control. For people who had lived a normal life, it must have been difficult—if not impossible—to understand what it meant for us to be told, "Get there early." It meant, "If you're late, it won't be there for you."

Men and women were separated, and Mama, Frydzia, and I went with the other women into a huge room where a voice over a loudspeaker instructed us to undress completely and leave our clothes on the floor. I was unhappy about getting undressed in public, but I worried more about losing my clothes. I wondered if they would still be there after the exam; the worry of possibly not finding my clothes made me feel even more undressed.

Frydzia and Lusia, Traunstein, Germany

Then we were instructed to line up according to the first letter of our surnames. Chaos ensued, as many women did not understand the instructions. For many, the whole scene evoked the worst possible memories of deportations and selections. Fortunately, the medical personnel—doctors, nurses, assistants—were all American, and that was comforting. The fear of German doctors was deeply ingrained in people's minds. We pushed our way to the M line, which moved slowly.

I began to feel cold. I noticed that some women held their arms firmly against their chests, as did I—partly out of the cold, partly because the strange thing about being naked is that you feel it most acutely when you have a sense of being observed. Many women around me were crying, clearly dealing with the terror this experience evoked. I did not fully understand their anxiety, but I had my own to deal with anyway. Besides, how do you understand such things when you're in the middle of it all? In retrospect, a simple piece of cloth to cover ourselves with would have made a tremendous difference emotionally.

As the line moved slowly, I grew more upset. I asked my mother to switch places with me so that I could hide behind her.

My turn came. The doctor, wearing glasses and a white coat, was kindly looking. He spoke softly, but I didn't understand; later, I realized that he spoke with a Southern drawl that put comprehension beyond the few English words I knew. I assumed he had asked my name, so I told him. But he just smiled and shook his head. For all I knew, he had said, "Hi, how are you?" or had asked if I had any ailments to report. What was clear was that he seemed to understand my anxiety; he seemed to have the capacity to appreciate the difficult circumstances we were in. He was careful not to look at me closely in a way that might embarrass me, and his examination was quick. I was grateful. He stamped some papers, which I assumed meant that I was healthy enough to go to America.

And then, it all almost unraveled. One of the processing requirements was a chest X-ray examining the lungs. No one with tuberculosis could enter the United States, so we all duly took the X-rays and waited for the results.

I will never forget the day they came. Mama, Papa, Frydzia were all okay—but not me. There was something wrong with my lungs. The bad news was entirely unexpected. I had been sick as a young child in Siberia with what we had always assumed was pneumonia. Could it possibly have been tuberculosis? In those days in Siberia, we never saw a doctor, and diagnoses were anybody's guess. You recovered from whatever illness you contracted, or you didn't. I had been very ill, but I recovered.

Now, the chest X-ray had discovered scar tissue in my lungs, and the US medical personnel were suspicious. Suddenly, it looked like we were not going to America after all.

My family was devastated. Mama appeared stunned; she always internalized everything without expressing her feelings. That is who she was, so different from Papa. Frydzia could not stop sobbing. There was such sadness all around. Beyond sadness, there was despair. It was in the air, palpable; you could almost touch it. I felt such guilt for having brought this on my family. All these years since the beginning of war, life had been filled with deprivation and lost dreams. To lose this final dream was unbearable. But my father would not be defeated.

That morning, Papa left our little room without saying anything. I learned later that there was a list with people's names posted on a bulletin board, on the exterior wall of the medical building. It was a list of names with suspicious X-ray results. Papa found my name prominently listed in alphabetical order for everyone to see. He couldn't bear to see my name listed among others not deserving a home in America! With anger in his heart and a pencil in his hand, Papa quickly crossed my name out, obliterating its very existence. But truth be told, at this time in our lives, he didn't much care if he was actually doing something that was prohibited or even against the law; he was angry and didn't want my name on the dreaded list.

When he got back, he found a terribly depressive atmosphere in our room. He looked at Frydzia and pressed his forefinger against his lips. "Shh," he said. "No more crying, do you hear me?" My sister looked up at him and stopped crying immediately. We were young, teenage girls, and Papa had a way of treating us as if we were still children. But that was okay. We knew how much he loved us.

Then he turned to me and pointed to the chair next to his. "Sorele, come sit here by me, and I will tell you a story." I sat. "You know the young man Yechiel, the son of the Great Rabbi?" I nodded my head; I thought I knew Yechiel.

"Well," said my father, "the Great Rabbi was killed in the *Horbin,* the Holocaust, may his soul rest in peace, but his son survived, and he is very smart, just like his father. Yechiel and I had a very interesting conversation this morning, and he gave me some very good advice. He said we should try to persuade the American medical people to let you take another chest X-ray. You know, when you stand in front of the big machine. And next time, nothing will show up in your lungs. Do you hear me?"

I nodded my head again.

Papa stood up and announced that he and I were taking a walk. I had no idea where we were going, but it didn't matter.

I loved getting out of the camp. We walked out the gate, and before long, we stood in front of a PX store set up by the armed forces exclusively for the US servicemen and their families. The US military personnel issued a special currency, called scrip, with which the servicemen could purchase nice things brought over from America. It was prohibited to sell or buy this currency, but Papa believed that some rules were made to be broken. He found a way to buy the forbidden currency. My guess is that it came from the black market.

I couldn't believe my eyes when we stepped inside the PX. I had never in my entire life seen such luxuries—counters and shelves full of candies, chocolates in gold and silver wrappings, boxes and baskets filled with candied fruit under colorful cellophane wrapping paper. There were toiletries, beautiful silk scarves, perfumes, and cigarettes. *All this*, I thought, *for the servicemen and their families.*

The man behind the counter seemed surprised to see us. After all, people like Papa in his shabby sport coat and a shy, young girl trailing behind were not his usual customers.

Papa approached the counter in his most dignified manner. He did not speak English at all, but someone had taught him to say the words he needed for this task. "Mister, mister, if you please,"—and Papa pointed at me—"fur mine daughter I vant buy Hershey shokolat."

Papa opened his hand, and there in his palm was the forbidden scrip. The man behind the counter looked at the scrip, looked at us, reached quickly behind the counter, and handed me a real Hershey chocolate bar. He took the scrip and gave us some change.

Without another word Papa turned around and, with his head held high, stepped out of the store, without a good-bye or a thank-you. I followed him out meekly. Papa had wanted to make me happy, but instead, I was embarrassed. I wanted desperately to make a good impression on the American who was kind to us. I guess I was too young to understand that what really mattered most was for Papa to retain some dignity. Maybe for that reason he didn't say another word. He was a proud man, but the war had forced him to beg when he needed to beg.

~

We sat on a bench, and I just stared at the chocolate bar in my hand. I felt the most awful conflict I had ever experienced. I wanted to taste the chocolate so badly, yet I felt that I needed to keep it for later, maybe share it with the rest of the family. Finally, I gave in to the temptation. I took one bite and then another. I was reluctant to chew it for fear that it would not last, so I let the chocolate melt in my mouth.

"Sorele, it's good?" Papa asked. I nodded my head and offered to share it with him. He just shook his head. "No, I don't really like chocolate that much," he said. Of course, he loved chocolate; I knew that. I finished the entire bar and then folded the wrapper and put it in my pocket for safekeeping and for good memories. I looked up at Papa's face. I think I was hoping for some approval for having eaten the entire chocolate all by myself. What I heard next truly amazed me. "Come," he said, "we will go back to the PX to get more chocolate."

This time as we entered the store, the man behind the counter actually smiled at us. Papa stretched out his hand again, and again, he said, "Mister, mister, if you please, Hershey shokolat, please." The man scooped up the scrip—I thought we shortchanged him—smiled, and with great flair, handed me another Hershey bar. This time, I did not eat the entire chocolate bar.

As we walked back to the camp, Papa and I had a very interesting conversation. Mostly, he spoke, and I listened. He elaborated on the benefits derived from eating chocolate. Trying to look very serious with his brows drawn together, he said that he knew from very reliable sources that the chocolate I just ate would actually "cover up and conceal those silly little scratches" in my lungs, and next time, the X-ray machine would find nothing "bad."

"Nothing at all, do you hear me?" he said. Even I couldn't believe such a silly story. I laughed so hard.

"Sorele, we are going to America, I promise you. Do you believe me?" he asked. I believed him, but not entirely.

The following week, Papa and I approached the American medical team with the assistance of a German–English translation service. I was so happy to see that it was the interpreter who was pleading on our behalf. I did not want Papa to have to beg again. The Americans looked at me, and they relented. I guess they took pity on us. The second chest X-ray showed the same scar tissue, but the doctors who reviewed the results very carefully determined that I did not suffer from any contagious disease. The scar tissue had been in my lungs a very long time.

Finally, we were told I would be allowed to go to America. I didn't know much about American people, but I was so moved by their kindness. I really believed that from that day on, I would love every American person I would ever meet.

We boarded a passenger train in the Munich rail station that was to take us to the North Sea port of Bremerhaven. From there, we would make the long voyage across the Atlantic on the *General C. H. Muir*, a troop transport vessel that would deposit us on the American shores, past the Statue of Liberty in New York harbor, on August 23, 1949.

On the train were hundreds of people like us, Holocaust survivors all going to America with a promise of a home. My family and I sat quietly in a small compartment with a window between two rows of seats. There was hardly any talk. We had long ago forsaken what seemed like superfluous chatter. There was no room for it in our lives, as if we had adopted a thrifty economy in everything in our lives, even the luxury of speech.

We were going to America. This was such a major event in our lives, it seemed almost sacrilegious to discuss it.

Mama and Papa seemed absorbed in their own thoughts. Mama especially wore a vacant, chilled look in her eyes. She sat by the window, her arms tightly wrapped around herself. I scrutinized their facial expressions, searching for signs of hope, something encouraging. It wasn't there. The hardships of almost ten years and the personal losses in their lives had aged them tremendously.

I thought I understood the ruination of our lives. Still, I dared to hope for something good in our future. We were going to our new home. Why did they always have to be so unhappy? I was determined not to become like that, not to let this depression happen. Pain had become part of our lives, that which I wanted to discard more than anything. Yes, I had been scarred, but I knew I would recover. I was certain I would find a better life in America.

I hated the gloom around me. I wanted to sit by myself, so I took a seat near a window, steps from the rest of the family. I felt peaceful watching the beautiful scenery spreading out in front of me. Things were moving, always changing, always appearing and disappearing like the very nature of our lives. The America I looked forward to was not the country famous for everything being the biggest, the tallest, and the grandest. Actually, what I kept thinking about was American people having a bathroom of their own inside their very own homes. It seemed unreal. There were so many things I had not yet experienced.

Going to America was the most wonderful event in our lives, and it was happening at last. Yet I felt sadness when I thought about the friends I had left behind. I felt particularly sad about a boy—actually a young man. Millek was going away to a medical school in Innsbruck, Austria. He was a distant relative of Tante Bronia and Uncle Beno. He also survived the war by being deported to Siberia.

After the war, he and our family lived in the same DP camp. He used to visit sometimes. I was fifteen and very shy. I don't believe I ever said two words in his presence. It was devastating to learn that he was going away. Sadly, this was the pattern of our lives. People were always going away.

But this was different. I knew that I had fallen in love for the first time in my life. In saying good-bye to him, I had my first kiss.

～

I stayed at the window for hours. Frydzia and Mama came by from time to time, just to check on me. I watched a lovely sunset. Then it grew dark. Suddenly, I heard a voice asking, "Would you like some coffee?" I looked up and saw a smiling face, a tall young man, maybe nineteen or twenty years old. He was holding a metal pot in one hand and two or three tin cups in the other.

Almost immediately, I felt drawn to him, to his tallness, the blond of his hair, the blue of his eyes. At first glance, he looked like the Aryan Germans, but instead of being afraid, I was fascinated by his looks.

Edward, Germany, 1949

I never drank coffee, but I thought if I said yes, he would stay a little longer. "Yes, I would like some coffee," I said, trying hard to sound mature and well mannered. I watched his slender, graceful fingers as he handed me a cup of coffee. I took one sip and almost choked on it. That brew was bitter. That is when the young man's charming smile became a resounding laugh. I liked that. God knows I needed a little laughter in my life. The young man sat down and introduced himself.

"My name is Edward, but most people call me Edek," he said.

"And I am called Lusia, but sometimes my father calls me Sorele, my Hebrew name," I replied.

Then, without a word, Edward excused himself. He was back a moment later, this time without the coffeepot. He sat down, which pleased me, and we started talking. Actually, he did most of the talking, while I mostly stared. I couldn't help feeling fascinated by his demeanor, the warmth in his eyes, and his smiling face. I didn't know it then, but this was exactly what I needed most—a young, smiling face. This vital young man couldn't possibly be a part of the bedraggled, seemingly lifeless people on the train. Who was he, and where did he come from? He was so different; there was energy and excitement about him. He spoke of America with such delight, and he was full of knowledge about the country he didn't know, the country that was to become his home as well.

Soon, he made himself comfortable in a seat across from me and began telling interesting, funny, fantastic adventure stories. He never took his eyes off me, and all the time, he insisted that the adventures had really happened and that the stories were really true. But, of course, he had never experienced any of them; he had only read about them. I didn't care if they were true or not. For a brief moment, I felt so happy.

It was very late. But it didn't matter, for this was an all-night train ride to the harbor. Edward and I stood near the door of the compartment, in full view of the other passengers and my family. Mama and Papa looked puzzled. Frydzia seemed intrigued—*What is my sister discussing with this total stranger, and why is she laughing so much?* I did not much care what anyone thought. I thought that I had met someone amusing and interesting and so handsome—someone who could become my friend.

My parents signaled to me to join them in their compartment. They clearly were not happy that I was speaking with a total stranger, someone I had not been introduced to. After all those years of upheaval, the long and difficult years of war that had upended our lives, they still held on to the old-world views. They believed very strongly that a young lady did not speak with strangers. But most of all, they wished that I would behave in a dignified manner. That was their wish for both Frydzia and me.

I had always been more persistent in doing things my

Frydzia, US immigration/affidavit photo

way; maybe I learned it from life or Papa. But Frydzia had always been more accommodating and complied with their wishes. She was the "perfect" daughter. She was the "perfect" young lady, and she was beautiful in a delicate sort of way. I was always envious of her beauty. Sometimes I heard people say that I was pretty. But my kind of "pretty" was different. My features were not as delicate and elegant as hers.

Now, my parents sensed that I was not willing to conform to their unique values.

Edward said good-night. With sadness in my heart, I watched him walk away. Papa was very unhappy with me. He made me promise I would not speak with strangers, at least not until we reached the American shores. He was very firm about it. I thought maybe I was having too much fun laughing and speaking with Edward—maybe that was something that unsettled my family. I felt very conflicted. I had always trusted their powers of reasoning. I was still so young. I knew there was much I needed to learn. Yet, for the first time ever, I knew that I would have to disregard my parents' wishes. This was stronger than anything I had felt before.

I hoped that Edward and his family and my family would all be boarding the same ship because I was convinced that I would see Edward again, speak with him, and enjoy his company again.

We boarded the troop transporting vessel *General C. H. Muir* on August 14, 1949, at the North Sea port of Bremerhaven, Germany. I watched as Edward, his parents, and his brother walked slowly up the ship's gangplank. My heart did a triple somersault! Now, I was certain we were to cross the Atlantic on the same ship. Nine days with Edward was happiness unimaginable. It was beyond any happiness I had ever experienced in my entire life. I was on my way to heaven, and I wasn't even asleep. This was real.

We boarded the ship. My family and his shook hands. Now, we were all introduced. I hoped Papa felt a little better. Edward actually had a family. I knew Papa would feel good that Edward came from what seemed like a solid family. And they were Jewish! That made things even better.

My parents wore very ordinary, unimpressive clothes; Papa wore his ancient sport coat and hat, and Mama wore her best dress (she was so skinny that the dress hung on her). Edward's parents wore tailored suits, which impressed my parents. This was another hurdle out of the way. Edward and his younger brother, Jacob, both wore pilot-style leather jackets. Edward was taking photographs with a Leica, a technologically advanced camera of the day.

I kept staring at his mother. Regina was a striking woman with red hair and beautiful blue eyes. My mother also had beautiful blue eyes, but she was a brunette. Edward's mother looked familiar. I was certain that I had met her or seen her before. I just couldn't remember where.

Later that day, I recalled where I had seen her. It was pure coincidence and a little sad, almost unreal. I saw Regina naked, where all of us—hundreds of women—were thrust together during our physical exams. It was her striking red hair that attracted my attention. She stood a little ahead of us on the same line, in the section for women whose surnames started with the letter *L*.

It seemed so sad to me that I should see her—the woman who years later became my mother-in-law—for the first time under such unfavorable circumstances, even before we met. Oh, how I wished that I had not seen her that day in the examination hall! In my mind, she had lost some of the dignity she deserved to keep. I tried very hard to erase that image. I vowed never to mention this to anyone.

Edward was very intelligent. He spoke five languages, including English. He taught himself rudimentary English by reading discarded or old copies of the *Herald Tribune* with the help of a borrowed English–German dictionary.

We got on board and, almost immediately, all men over the age of eighteen were informed that they were required to put in certain number of work hours each day; that was to pay for the passage. Being multilingual, Edward became an interpreter. His job was to assign work to other men.

Edward assigned chimney painting to my father along with other men. I was horrified!

"How could you do such a thing, placing my father all the way up there to paint a chimney?" I screamed. That was our first fight on board. Edward's answer astounded me and got me rooted in my tracks.

He said very calmly, "Painting the chimney will not hurt your father. And being high up there, he may gain a better perspective on life."

Then, with a tiny smile and a little wink in his eye, he said, "Besides, how else would I be able to romance his daughter?"

I was speechless. Then I laughed. Later, I learned that he had assigned a kitchen job, several decks below, to a young man I knew only vaguely from one of the DP camps. Karol (in America, he became Carl) sometimes smiled at me and said hello. Even from several decks below, Karol managed to sneak out of the kitchen, along with smuggled grapefruits. I had learned to enjoy that fruit very much, after all.

Eating in the mess hall was an adventure I also enjoyed. I guess everything was an adventure because everything was new. After supper, we watched American-made films. I didn't much care for war films. But I liked films with lots of romantic scenes. I guess I was a normal sixteen-year-old teenager with romance in my heart.

I liked dancing too. Soft lights illuminated the entire dance hall, creating a pleasant, even a romantic environment. Edward and I danced to popular tunes. He held me ever so gently, while we danced slowly among many young people. I recall feeling emotionally moved as we danced to a tune called "Begin the Beguine." After all these years, I still remember the words.

When they begin the beguine
It brings back the song of music so tender
It brings back the night of tropical splendor …

To this day, the voyage to America remains the most memorable experience of my life.

Epilogue

Early morning about 6:00 a.m. on August 23, 1949, before reaching New York Harbor, we glimpsed the Statue of Liberty for the first time.

People crowded the decks, taking up every last inch of space. With wonder and shedding tears, people kept saying over and over, "Look, look, there she is—the Statue of Liberty."

My family and I stood quietly at the railing. Frydzia and I, in our best summer dresses, stood side by side, holding hands. After all these years, I still remember what we wore. Frydzia's dress was of thin, flowered fabric draped softly around her beautiful, shapely body. And I remember clearly the dress I wore to greet the Statue of Liberty. It had green and white stripes, puffy, short sleeves, a lovely but rather risqué scooped neckline, and it was tight around my narrow waist with a flared skirt.

Papa was smiling at the sight of the lady in the harbor. No, he was actually laughing with joy. It had been so long since I'd seen him smiling or laughing. He was so happy. But Mama had tears in her eyes; that was her way of feeling happy.

I had never seen a photograph of the Statue of Liberty. But this exceeded my expectation. The statue was grander and by far more beautiful than I had imagined.

"This is where it all begins for us. This is where our home will be forever," Papa said.

Then he reached into the pocket of his old, shabby sport coat and withdrew a fistful of American money!

"You see this money? Thirty-six American dollars!" He went on to explain, "Thirty-six is two times eighteen. In Jewish tradition, even back in ancient times, the number eighteen was and still is to this day symbolic for life and good fortune. Thirty-six means that it's twice as good!"

I had no idea my father had American money in his pocket. I was even a little apprehensive. After all, we weren't even Americans yet and already he had in his possession American money!

Then he said, "With this money, we will start a brand-new life here, and we will work hard and not ask for a handout."

We disembarked with the help of the crew and the Joint, the members of the American Jewish Joint Distribution Committee. They were so helpful. They literally took our family by our hands and delivered us straight into the open arms of Uncle Jack and his wife, Tante Ida.

It was heart-wrenching watching Uncle Jack holding Papa, his younger brother, tight in his arms, both crying. They had not seen each other in more than thirty-five years since Uncle Jack (Jacob in the old country) departed from Poland when he was hardly a teenager and my father was just a little boy.

After all those years of corresponding and trying so hard to bring us over, it all became real, and Uncle Jack became real. It was a joyful reunion.

I had not seen Edward or any of his family that morning of the sighting of the Statue of Liberty. I was hoping to say a proper good-bye. I looked around. I thought I had seen him in a distant corner, far from where my family gathered.

The huge holding compound in New York Harbor was filled to capacity with hundreds of immigrants, all searching for friends or families. I could hardly discern Edward's familiar face in the midst of all those people. Edward and his family were being greeted by their own American family.

During the ocean crossing, Edward had told me that he and his family would most probably be staying with his aunt and uncle in Pittsburgh, Pennsylvania.

We shook hands and said good-bye. I tried hard not to show any emotions, but Edward must have seen tears in my eyes. He inched a little closer and kissed me on the lips. We made a promise to each other that we would write and meet again soon.

"I will come to see you soon, Lucynka," he said.

"Why do you call me that? That is not my name," I said.

Edward smiled and said, "That is my pet name for you."

In all my sixteen years, I had experienced many painful good-byes. It had become a deep-rooted part of my life. But Edward's departure was different. It was the pinnacle of all I had lost in the ten years since the beginning of the war. It was shattering. And I didn't even have a picture of Edward's smiling face. I vowed to remember his face.

Uncle Jack and Tante Ida welcomed my family into their home in Bensonhurst, a pleasant Italian and Jewish neighborhood in Brooklyn, New York. My aunt, uncle, and cousins Aaron and Irving made room for us in their modest rental apartment. They made room for us in their home and their hearts. They fed us and kept us under their roof for more than one month.

In September, only several weeks after coming to America, Papa went to work in Uncle Jack's business, plating and polishing costume jewelry. It was hard labor, especially working in conditions that required hot water and very high temperatures.

He loved working with his brother and his two nephews. Aaron and Irving adored their uncle Abe. Papa had reached the age of forty-eight. He was still very handsome in spite of long years of hardships and tribulation. His nephews wished to look like him because of his full head of dark brown hair (their father had a receding hairline). They kept telling Papa that he resembled the actor James Mason, and Papa would say, "Who is James Mason?"

In September, only weeks after our arrival in the United States, I enrolled into tenth grade in Lafayette High School, a school in my uncle's neighborhood.

At first, I had some difficulty with the English language and adjusting in general. Eventually, I made some friends but not entirely. More than wanting friends, I needed to belong. But that was not so simple. The only thing we all had in common was our age as fifteen- and sixteen-year-olds.

But I was different and felt like an outsider. I couldn't discuss my life's experiences; I didn't think anyone would understand. So I rejected friendship, even when it was offered to me in good spirit.

I remember a girl in one of my classes saying, "Why don't you wear some lipstick? It would look good on you." I didn't think about lipstick. I hated the differences between me and the other students who seemed to have such perfect lives. I felt ashamed of what my life had been like and where I came from.

What I didn't understand at the time was that being different was not such a bad thing. But most of all, I didn't understand that we were a product of our lives' experiences. And that too was not such a bad thing.

Mama stayed home. That was when we had already moved into our own small, two-bedroom apartment, a walk-up "railroad flat" in the Brownsville section of Brooklyn, not far from Uncle Jack and Tante Ida.

Mama cooked and cleaned and communicated with neighbors who would converse with her in Yiddish and taught her how to shop for food in America. Eventually, Mama went to night school and learned to speak English and, much later, read the *New York Times*. She was proud of that achievement.

At eighteen, Frydzia found a job sewing thick-gauge plastic material on heavy industrial sewing machines. Hers was the most exhausting job. Sometimes she came home after a long day's work so tired that she would go straight to sleep without dinner. She earned seventy-five cents per hour, minimum wage in those days, but it was hardly enough to pay rent on the apartment, food, and utilities. Even with Papa's wages, it wasn't enough.

I dropped out of high school only six weeks after I enrolled. My high school counselor tried hard to talk me out of quitting school. She said I had a bright future if I would only continue with my education. I explained that I needed to work and promised that, one day, I would go back to school and get my education. I didn't think she believed me.

I sometimes think back to those high school days of mine. Did I in fact leave school for altruistic reasons—wanting to help my family financially—or was it something else? Perhaps I was compelled to leave school because I didn't feel that I belonged ...

My work was tedious and boring, packing and shipping goods in a stockroom, also at the minimum wage of seventy-five cents per hour. That is when I understood I needed to break out of that mold, and that education was my ticket to a better life.

Many years later, I fulfilled my promise; I did go back to school. Doing undergraduate and graduate work was a very lengthy process. Juggling family responsibilities, home, and children, it was exhausting and a financial struggle. It took many years of both day and evening classes.

I earned a bachelor of arts degree from the City University of New York and a postgraduate degree, a master of arts in occupational therapy, from New York University. In fact, when applying to a postgraduate school, I was accepted to the same program in both Columbia University and New York University. I chose New York University because of the proximity to home.

Years later, my big sister, Frydzia, also went back to school part time. She earned a bachelor of arts degree from the City University of New York.

But all that was a long time off. In the meantime, during the difficult months late in 1949, I could not have foreseen all the good that still awaited me.

One winter evening, there was a knock on the door, and there was Edward standing in our doorway, smiling his beautiful smile, his eyes shining with happiness. I almost fainted from surprise. I flew into his arms, wrapping my arms around him.

Edward liked New York better than Pittsburgh and decided to stay. He lived with a great-aunt in Brooklyn. We dated on and off. Sometimes we dated other people, but eventually, we became a couple.

Edward found a job at Ohrbach's, a department store in New York City. He worked in the stockroom and worked very hard. People who spoke English with an accent were not generally hired to provide services to customers from behind the sales counter.

Edward also went back to school. He earned an undergraduate degree and a master's degree in business administration from Baruch College of the City University of New York.

Edward and I married when I was not quite nineteen. We raised a family—a girl and a boy.

From the very beginning, our children understood that knowledge, education, and hard work held the key to a better and meaningful life. And, here in America, all that was possible. Our children also hold advanced degrees, and they are very successful. But best of all, they are good people.

After all, Papa was right when he said, "Anything is possible if you work hard. You can achieve anything in America."